TURKEY'S
HIGH MOUNTAINS
AND SKI RESORTS

by
İsmet ÜLKER

❖⋙❋⋘❖

REPUBLIC OF TURKEY
MINISTRY OF CULTURE AND TOURISM PUBLICATIONS

© Ministry of Culture and Tourism of Republic of Turkey
General Directorate of Libraries and Publications
3324

Handbook Series
16

ISBN: 978-975-17-3581-2

www.kulturturizm.gov.tr
e-mail: yayimlar@kulturturizm.gov.tr

Translated by
Amy Spangler, Adnan Tonguç

Printed by
Atlas Printing Center
İvedik OSB 600. Sokak No:8 Yenimahalle-Ankara
Tel: 0 312 394 81 49 - Faks: 0312 394 81 50
www.atlasmat.com

First Edition
Print run: 5000.

Printed in Ankara in 2011.

Ülker, İsmet
    Turkey's High Mountains and Ski Resorts / İsmet Ülker; Trans:
Amy Spangler .- Ankara: Ministry of Culture and Tourism, 2011.

    174 p.: col. ill.; 20 cm.- (Ministry of Culture and
Tourism Publications; 3324. Handbook Series of
General Directorate of Libraries and Publications: 16)
    ISBN: 978-975-17-3581-2

    I. title. II. Spangler, Amy. III. Series
796.522

CONTENTS

İsmet ÜLKER

(Born 18th April 1940, Elazığ)

After high school, İsmet Ülker studied Physical Geography and Geology. In 1966 he became the Founding President of the Mountaineering Federation, and later in 1972-76 served as the President of the Ski Federation. Ülker served as Project Director, Department Chief and Vice General Director within the Ministry of Tourism and as Tourism Attaché in the diplomatic service.

İsmet Ülker initiated and managed the first planning activities for ski centres on the Uludağ, Köroğlu, Erciyes, Palandöken, Sarıkamış and Davraz mountain ranges. As a member of the national skiing team, he took part in the 1974 St. Moritz World Skiing Championship and in the 1976 XII Innsbruck Winter Olympics. In addition to all of this, he carried out studies at the ski centres of St. Anton and Saalbach in Austria, and at the Zermatt Ski Centre of Switzerland. İsmet Ülker wrote specialised sources books on Medical Tourism, works on "Our Mountains", fiction and a collection of short stories titled Dağlarda Kırk Yıl (Forty Years on the Mountains) and Dağ Yeli Sarsık Eser (The Mountain Breeze Blows Shakily).

The mountain will not come to you,
it is You who has to go to the mountains.
The mountain will not come to us,
it is Us who have to go to the mountains...

SKIING AND MOUNTAINEERING
ALL THROUGH THE YEAR IN TURKEY...

Dedicated to those for whom
mountains are their love and beloved...

Turkey, which is located on the middle latitudes of the northern hemisphere, is a Mediterranean country where high mountains and mid-altitude mountains covered with forests occupy vast areas.

The Rize - Kaçkar Mountains (3932 m.) located on the Northern Anatolian mountain range, the Taurus Aladağ Mountains (3771 m.) which are within the winding Taurus range along the southern part of the Anatolian Peninsula, the Hakkari - Cilo and Sat Mountains (4136 m.) that are part of the Southeastern Tauruses, and volcanic mountains like the Kayseri - Mount Erciyes (3917 m.) and Greater Ararat Mountain (5137 m.), make up Turkey's high altitude mountainous areas.

Turkey's most important ski centres are Mount Uludağ (2543 m.) above Bursa and Mount Köroğlu (2400 m.) near Bolu which are mid-altitude and forested, as well as Erciyes (3917 m.) near Kayseri, Palandöken (3176 m.) near Erzurum, Sarıkamış (2634 m.) near Kars, Davraz (2635 m.) near Isparta and Kastamonu's Ilgaz (2587 m.) mountains.

Both the high altitude mountainous areas and the mid-altitude mountainous and forested areas of Turkey are suitable for both mouintaneering and winter sports, hence welcome visitors all year-round. Under normal weather conditions these areas get more than two metres of snowfall in the winter. The Anatolian peninsula generally has sunny, blue, unclouded skies in summer and winter, making Turkey an attractive destination for both summer ascents and winter activities.

Shown here are Turkey's high mountains and main ski centres where winter sports take place all year-round... This is Greater Ararat Mountain, that wonder of Turkish and European geography and mountain of legends...

I would like to thank the General Directorate of Libraries and Publications that led to the preparation of this original work presenting the unique natural beauty and rich biodiversity of Turkey's high mountains, as well as its winter sports centres, most of which are located amidst forested areas.

MOUNTAINEERING AND
WINTER SPORTS IN TURKEY

In Turkey, mountaineering and winter sports began to acquire importance after 1923, following the foundation of the Republic. Skiing equipment imported from Sweden was sent to provincial centres like Kayseri, Elazığ, Erzurum, Kars and Bursa where there were "Halkevleri" (Houses of the People), thus encouraging the participation of young people in winter sports. It was within this context that in 1936 the "Mountaineering and Winter Sports Federation" was first established and Turkey took part with its team in the winter olympics held in Garmisch, Germany, that same year. Latif Osman Çıkıgil was appointed the first president of the Mountaineering and Winter Sports Federation, which in 1939 was turned into a state body. In 1943 Nizamettin Kırşan took Latif Osman Çıkıgil's place, and then in 1944, Asım Kurt, who had been trained in mountaineering and winter sports in Switzerland for two years, became the third president of the federation.

In 1937, a committee from the University of Berlin led by Dr. Hans Bobek, toured the Cilo and Sat mountains in Hakkari, conducting a study of their physical geography. This expedition was followed in 1949 by Dr. Blumenthal's studies of the Greater Ararat. As for the writer of this book, physical geographer and geologist İsmet Ülker, he held in 1962-63 a seminar titled "The Morphology of the Hakkari-Cilo Mountains", and in 1964 he wrote his graduate thesis on "Vulcanism and Vulcanic Shapes of Greater Ararat"*.

Physical Geographer Dr. Reşat İzbırak from the University of Ankara took part in the first of these expeditions to the Hakkari-Cilo mountains, while the second expedition saw the participation of Dr. Sırrı Erinç from the University of Istanbul. The first official ascent up Greater Ararat took place in 1954, and for the second time in 1956. Outstanding mountaineers took part in these ascents: Gültekin Çeki in the first and then Dr. Bozkurt Ergör, Ersin Alok and Engin Kongar in the second.

The national skiing team, trained by Austrian coaches, competed in the winter olympics of 1948, of 1956 and in all subsequent olympic games thereafter.

---

* This is the first scientific study of Greater Ararat carried out by Turkish citizens.

On 16th August 1963, the first Turkish female mountaineers to climb Greater Ararat (5137 m.) were Gülay Albayrak of the Elazığ Mountaineering Team led by İsmet Ülker, and Yıldız Değirmencioğlu of the Manisa Mountaineering Team led by Erdoğan Dayıoğlu. In 1966, the Mountaineering and Winter Sports Federation was split into two federations; one for "Mountaineering" and the other for "Skiing". İsmet Ülker was appointed president of the Mountaineering Federation, but he preferred to remain a "founding president", and made it possible for Latif Osman Çıkıgil to be appointed president of the Mountaineering Federation for a second time.

In 1972, İsmet Ülker was appointed president of the Skiing Federation, and in 1973, Dr. Bozkurt Ergör was appointed president of the Mountaineering Federation. During and after this period, importance and precedence was given to the popularisation of skiing and to the training of outstanding sportspeople, while in mountaineering, "winter climbing" was preferred over "summer climbing".

The first winter ascents were led by Dr. Bozkurt Ergör. Following the first winter ascents of the mountains of Erciyes (3917 m.), of Demirkazık (3758 m.) on the Taurus - Aladağlar range and of Mount Kaldı (3725 m.), Dr. Bozkurt Ergör became on the first mountaineer in the world to reach the summit of the Greater Ararat (5137 m.) on the 21st February 1970. In 1973 a four member national skiing team (two Alpine skiers and two nordic skiers) led by İsmet Ülker for the first time ascended Greater Ararat on skis and came back down skiing. Between 1972 and 1976, the Turkish National Skiing Team took part in the 1974 Kitzbühel "descent", the St. Moritz Alpine skiing and the Sweden Falun nordic skiing championships, as well as in the 1976 Innsbruck Winter Olympics.

After 1976, federation presidents changed frequently, but then Alaattin Karaca was appointed president of the Mountaineering Federation in 1997 and Dr. Özer Ayık was appointed president of the Skiing Federation in 2005, positions which they currently continue to hold.

After 1983, trained mountaineers from Middle East Technical University (ODTÜ) and Bilkent University, both in Ankara, began to carry out high altitude and advanced mountaineering activities. For the "2002 World Year of Mountains", the ODTÜ-ORDOS Mountaineering Team led by Serhan Poçan, made up of 5 female and 7 male mountaineers, successfully completed the north - south winter ascent for the first time ever, as part of an endeavor called "Trans-Ararat". In 2005 and 2006, the same team first ascended Gasherbrum II Peak (8035 m.) and then, Mount Everest (8848 m.) in the Himalaya Mountains.

Similarly Nasuh Mahruki, who is a pioneer of Turkish mountaineering, ascended Everest with Dr.Yılmaz Sevgül, first in 1995 and then again in 2010, while in 2000 he climbed the world famous "K2" Peak (8616 m.). Another Turkish mountaineer, Tunç Fındık, managed to climb to Everest's summit twice, the first time being in 2001. The winter sports and skiing activities with the widest scope among those held in Turkey were the "Universiade-Erzurum 2011 Winter Olympics". A total of 600 Million TL was spent on these activities.

These activities were organised and carried out thanks to the precious contributions of Dr. Özer Ayık, President of the Turkish Skiing Federation, and his colleagues; the administrators of the Turkish Universities Sports Federation; Bekir Korkmaz, chairman of the organising committee; Fatih Çıntımar, the Erzurum Provincial Director for Youth and Sports Affairs, and his colleagues; and the members and ski instructors of the national team.

Nowadays in Turkey there are around 500,000 people who practice mountaineering and winter sports, the majority being comprised of skiers. There are a total of around 20,000 licensed and unlicensed hotel beds in the skiing centres of Uludağ, Kartalkaya, Davraz, Erciyes, Palandöken and Sarıkamış, which are Turkey's most important skiing centres.

The Turkish Mountaineering Federation, which has given increasing importance to advanced mountaineering since 2009, now manages 817 mountaineering clubs in 79 provinces, and as of 2010, 6,100 women and 18,400 men were active in these clubs, as licensed sportspeople.

Turkey's high mountains and ski centres are open for excursions and studies by mountain and nature lovers, and for mountaineering and winter sports activities. It is only the Hakkari-Cilo and Sat mountains in the area close to the border of Iraq and Iran that are "restricted areas" for security reasons. As for the ascents of Greater Ararat, an application for a permit has to be presented either directly or through travel agencies to a diplomatic mission of Turkey, and the ascent has to be done under the supervision of a certified guide.

Turkey's high mountains, where you can ski all through the year, its ski centres surrounded by forests, and Greater Ararat, that masterpiece and highest summit of the geography of Turkey and Europe, with its legends and Noah's ark, with its high glaciers, its noble-spirited people and flowers, all await mountain- and nature-lovers.

MOUNTAINS

Their smokey summits scraping the sky, Wavy mountains woven with seven colours, Leaning on each other, Holding hands, Mountains extending from time immemorial to eternity

Song in the Hüseyni mode

Composed by: M. Nurettin SELÇUK

Lyrics: Vecdi BİNGÖL

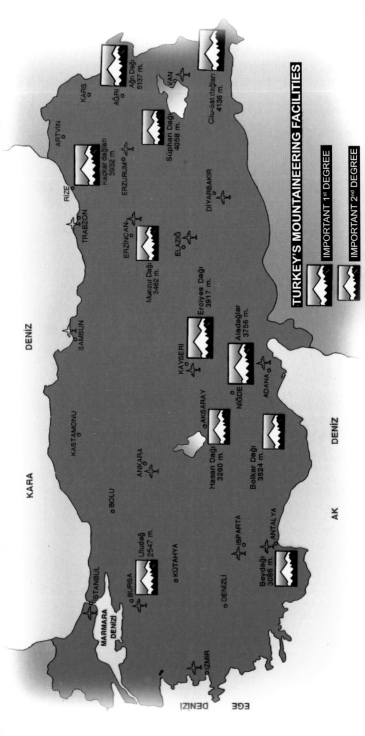

TURKEY'S MOUNTAINEERING FACILITIES

IMPORTANT 1st DEGREE

IMPORTANT 2nd DEGREE

KARA
DENİZ

AK DENİZ

MARMARA DENİZİ

EGE DENİZİ

İSTANBUL
BURSA
KÜTAHYA
DENİZLİ
İZMİR
ISPARTA
ANTALYA
BOLU
KASTAMONU
ANKARA
SAMSUN
TRABZON
RİZE
ARTVİN
KARS
AĞRI
ERZURUM
ERZİNCAN
ELAZIĞ
DİYARBAKIR
VAN
KAYSERİ
NİĞDE
AKSARAY
ADANA

Uludağ 2547 m.
Beydağı 3086 m.
Hasan Dağı 3260 m.
Bolkar Dağı 3524 m.
Aladağlar 3756 m.
Erciyes Dağı 3917 m.
Munzur Dağı 3462 m.
Kaçkar dağları 3932 m.
Ağrı Dağı 5137 m.
Suphan Dağı 4058 m.
Cilo-Sat dağları 4136 m.

TURKEY'S TECTONIC STRUCTURE AND THE FORMATION OF ITS HIGH MOUNTAINS

The area presently occupied by Turkey solidified into earth from north to south. In other words, while the layers of Nothern Anatolia were formed during the Primary Period, the layers of Southern Anatolia covered by the Taurus mountain range were formed during the Tertiary Period. Turkey's land consists of four main structures,. Though unique to Turkey, the formation of these structures is connected to the movements responsible for the formation of the Alpine - Himalaya mountain ranges as well. The following is a summary of these tectonic structures, which can be said to comprise the foundation and roof of the formation of Turkey itself.

The Northern Anatolia Range Belt:

The mountain ranges on this tectonic belt are also known as the "Pontids". In the western part of this belt there are the Istranca Mountains (1000 m.) with a low altitude and the structure of a massif. In its central part there are the Bolu Köroğlu Mountain (2400 m.) and the Ilgaz Mountains (2587 m.). In the Central Black Sea Area there are the Karagöl Mountains (3100 m.) while further east there are the Rize - Kaçkar Mountains (3632 m.).

The Central Anatolia Massif Belt:

The Central Anatolia and Eastern Anatolia series of volcanoes rise above this belt of massifs known as the Anatolids. Within the Central Anatolia series of volcanoes there are high volcanic mountains like the Erciyes (3917 m.) and Hasan (3268 m.) mountains, while within the Eastern Anatolia series of volcanoes there are the Greater Ararat (5137 m.), Tendürek (3533 m.), (4058 m.) and Nemrut (3050 m.) mountains.

The Southern Anatolia Range Belt:

These twisting mountain ranges all along the southern side of the Anatolian peninsula, called the Taurus Mountains, make up the 3rd tectonic segment of Turkey. In the western part of this range called also the "Taurids" there are the Beydağları (3070 m.) mountains, while the Bolkar Mountains (3524 m.) and the Aladağlar (3756 m.) mountains rise above its central part. Further on from the Aladağlar there are the Tahtalı (3075 m.), Binboğa (2945 m.) and Munzur (3462 m.) mountains.

The South-eastern Anatolia Range Belt:

This belt of mountains consists of the South-eastern Taurus Mountains, and is made up of the Amanos Mountains and Nurhak Mountains. It continues as the Malatya-Beydağları (2600 m.), the Elazığ-Hazarbaba mountain (2350 m.) and the Mastar Mountains. Through Bitlis it extends to Hakkari and from there to Iran. At the far eastern end of these mountains there are the Hakkari - Cilo and Sat mountains (4136 m.).

Following this preliminary information, we shall describe separately Turkey's mountainous areas that are important from the point of view of mountain sports and mountain tourism, and its mid-altitude mountainous and forested areas.

THE GREATER ARARAT (5137 m.)

The Greater Ararat (5137 m.), which is Turkey's highest peak, is an extinct volcano. This mountain, rising within the Eastern Anatolian series of volcanoes, is located at the point where the Turkish-Ira n and Nakhchivan borders meet. To the south-east of the Greater Ararat volcano there is the Lesser Ararat (3896 m.), which also is an extinct volcano. In between the Greater and the Lesser Ararat volcanoes, there is the "Serdarbulak plateau". This lava plateau connecting the two extinct volcanoes, has an average height of 2600 m.

The Greater Ararat (5137 m.), rising in between the Plain of Iğdır (840 m.) to its north and the Plain of Doğubeyazıt (1640 m.) to its south, has a majestic look resulting from its high elevation. The first ascent up the Greater Ararat was carried out in September 1829 by A. von Parrot, while the first winter ascent up this mountain was completed on 21st February 1970 by Dr. Bozkurt Ergör.

The Ararat is famous throughout the world, as a result of its being quoted in the sacred books in the Great Flood and Noah's Ark legends.[1]

The Formation of the Greater Ararat: Its Structure and Geology

The Greater Ararat, which is Turkey's highest mountain (5137 m.), is an extinct volcano. The Greater Ararat is situated on a base with a diameter of around 55 km. along its NW-SE axis, and of around 30 km. along its NS-SW axis. It is a "stratovolcano" with a single ejection conduit and with layers formed by central eruption.[2]

At the southeast of the Greater Ararat, at a distance of around 11-12 km., there is the Lesser Ararat Volcano (3896 m.), and in between them there is the Serdarbulak lava plateau and around the Biçare Mountain minor volcano cones resulting from secondary eruptions. The "Ararat Volcano System" made up of the Greater Ararat, the Lesser Ararat and of the Biçare coneswas formed in five main stages of volcanic activity. In the first stage, the Greater Ararat came into being by ejecting pyroclastic flows (volcanic tuff, pebbles and projectiles); in the second stage, it ejected andesite; and in third, it ejected basaltic lava and tuff.

---

1 "Ararat" was the name in Hebrew of the Urartu people, who lived in Eastern Anatolia in the 9th century BC.
2 Volcanoes, the lava flows of which accumulate on top of one another in a regular way, thus forming a chronological order, are called "stratovolcanoes".

(The volcanic strata in the landslide valley to the north of the mountain reflect these stages).

During the fourth stage when andesite lava was ejected by means of central eruptions, the Greater Ararat reached more or less its present day look. The Lesser Ararat Volcano (3896 m.) made up of andesite lava ejected separately was formed in this stage.

From time to time, there are earthquakes of a volcanic or tectonic origin in this area. For example, as a result of an earthquake that occurred in 1940, rocks and ice blocks came to be detached from the northern slope of the Greater Ararat (Abich, 1845). According to some studies, an "eruption of hot water" resulted in a great landslide, which formed the deep Cehennemdere valley, and the present day village of Yenidoğan was founded in place of the village of Ahora destroyed during this landslide.

As for the Lesser Ararat (3896 m.), which is devoid of glaciers and year-round snows, the crater has disappeared as a result of erosion, break up through freezing and filling up.

In conclusion, both the Greater and the Lesser Ararat's volcanic activities began in the second half of the Tertiary Period, in the late Neogene, continued in the Quaternary Period and having now ended, they are both extinct volcanoes.

The Morphology of Glaciers on the Greater Ararat

The Greater Ararat is Turkey's most important and interesting area from the point of view of the formation and morphology of glaciers. The top of Ararat is covered by a thick kind of glacier called an ice cap. This ice cap glacier, which in places has a thickness of tens of metres and is embedded over the crater, extends through the gorges between the central and western peaks of Ararat, downwards and towards the south, the southwest and the northwest. These glaciers that cover the flat top of the mountain follow the decline of the slopes, downwards, acquiring the characteristics of valley glaciers, and extend for 3500 metres towards the northwest.

The location and positions of the ice cap embedded on the Greater Ararat and of the valley glaciers branching out from this ice cap have been indicated on the map.

The big, thick blocks hanging out from the summit of Ararat, towards the north, break from a height of around 4500-4600 metres and fall into the Cehennem (Hell) Valley. These masses of ice, weighing tonnes, accumulate along the deep landslide valley of a length of around 8-10 km., creating a new "valley glacier".

This valley glacier covered in parts with broken rocks is a regenerated glacier or nucleus glacier. In places it is as thick as 20 metres and has a length of around 5 km. It has the characteristics of a valley glacier, and its lower end extends down to an altitude of 2500 metres.

Another noteworthy glacier area on the Greater Ararat is the Ülkeroğlu Glacier, also known as the Southern Glacier, and its surroundings.

The "Ülkeroğlu Glacier", with an altitude of 4900 - 5000 metres, is detached from the ice cap by means of width-wise crevasses, and having been formed by means of the erosion of the glacier's downwards flow from the flat summit, is embedded in a young glacier valley. The Ülkeroğlu Glacier, which is a typical valley glacier, has, as a result of the differences in hardness and inclination of the layers of lava, created three glacier balconies, and three glacier steps.[3]

The Ülkeroğlu Glacier or "Southern Glacier", the lower parts of which are in places covered with sand-pebbles and bigger stones, ends at an altitude of around 4000 metres. In front of the glacier there is an active moraine barrier. On the south-eastern and eastern sides of Ararat there is year-round snow and frozen snow also at altitudes lower than 4000 metres.

There are not many glacier lakes on the Greater Ararat. There is a single lake, the "Küp Gölü", on the north-west slope of the mountain, at an altitude of around 3450 metres. It is not clear whether this lake, which is round and deep, is a secondary conduit crater lake or a cirque lake.

The Water Situation: "Hydrology"

Due to their structural characteristics, volcanic areas and volcanoes are important from the point of view of surface and underground water flows. It is for this reason that also the Greater Ararat and its surrounding area has its own type of hydrological conditions and order. The glaciers embedded on the Greater Ararat serve as water stockage for the near environs of the mountain. This notwithstanding, there are almost no streams or lakes on Ararat (except for Küp Gölü).

When İsmet Ülker climbed 5 times to the summit of the Greater Ararat, his first ascent being in 1961, and most recently in 1966. İsmet Ülker, who was the first to study the Southern Glacier during his ascents of the Ararat in 1963 and in 1964, and who wrote a undergraduate thesis on this subject, found that the length of the glacier was around 5 km., while its thickness varied between 30 and 40 metres, and named the glacier "Ülkeroğlu".

The water from the melting glaciers, which cover the top of the Greater Ararat and which extend down to an altitude of 3500 m. on its north-western slopes, and down to 4000 m. on its southern slopes, seep under the extremely porous basaltic and andesite lavas, follow gravitation and the topographical inclination, and descend towards the base of the surrounding plains as "unbounded aquifers". This underground water, which flows according to the inclination of the area, flows towards the surrounding plains and at times forms underground streams.

These underground streams fed by melting snow, year-round snow and glaciers, surface as water sources with great pressure, and in general this happens in the valley floors where the layers of lava have ended, and in the areas of contact between volcanic stones and non-porous sedimentary rocks. The abundance of these streams changes according to the periods of melting and growing of the year-round snows, and they are at their most abundant in June and July.

These abundant sources with plenty of water, which are fed by the Greater Ararat's frozen snows and glaciers, surface in function of the extension of both glaciers and lava layers, near Karabulak, Topçatan and Çiftlik Village to the south of the mountain, and in Iğdır - Bulakbaşı, Aralık and in the location near the Turco-Iran border known as "Fountain of Süreyya" to the north of the mountain. These sources which possess plentiful water are called "bulak" in the area, i.e., Karabulak, Kanlıbulak, Serdarbulak, Sarıbulak etc. These plentiful underground water sources are used to irrigate the Plain of Iğdır, which has a microclimate, and where cotton is grown.

Natural Botanic Growth and Wildlife "flora and fauna"

The parts of the Greater Ararat up to an altitude of three-thousand metres are covered with summer pastures (yayla), and the parts between three-thousand metres and the limit of "year-round snow" (4000 m.) are covered with "high altitude meadows".

There is not much forest on Ararat. There are only scattered tree groups on the Korhan Plateau on the north-western slope of the Greater Ararat (5137 m.) and on the northern and western parts of the Lesser Ararat (3896 m.), and other forest like groups of trees consisting of birches (Betula) and oaks (Quercus).

The fauna of the Greater Ararat is quite varied. In its higher parts wolves and bears predominate. These are followed by the argali or mountain sheep (Ovis ammon anatolica). And in the hot and sandy areas where mountain slopes and plains join, there are snakes. In addition to these, many types of wild birds have found a suitable environment in the reed marshes and lakes to the north and south of the Greater Ararat, while the high plateaus are the preferred environment of the Caspian Snowcock (Tetraogallus caspius).

Climatic Conditions and Climbing Seasons:

There is a "continental" climate on the Greater Ararat rising in between the Upper Murat Basin and the Aras Basin in Eastern Anatolia, and in the area surrounding it. In this climate, summers will in general be sunny, hot and dry, while winter and spring will be rainy. In areas with a higher altitude, the altitude combined with low temperatures will lead to winter precipitations manifesting themselves as "snowfall".

The climatic values concerning the Doğubeyazıt skiing station to the south of the Greater Ararat, and of the Iğdır station to its north have been indicated in the following tables.

Name of the Station: Doğubeyazıt
Altitude: 1585 m.

	I	II	III	IV	V	VI	VII	VIII	IX	X	XI	XII	Yıl
Average monthly temperature (C°)	-5	-5	2	7	14	18	22	22	17	10	5	2	9
Sunny and partially sunny days/month	23	22	22	23	26	19	31	31	29	26	25	24	31
Average number of snow-covered days/month	15	20	7	-	-	-	-	-	-	-	1	9	52
Greatest thickness of snow-cover (cm.)	19	30	29	10	-	-	-	-	-	13	4	13	30
Average monthly relative humidity	71	71	67	62	59	53	46	51	51	64	68	72	61

Source: Bulletin of the State General Directorate of Meteorological Affairs.

These climatic conditions typical of the Greater Ararat, are important for both summer and winter ascents, but especially for winter ascents, because of the extreme ice formation and unpredictable weather conditions in winter. The most appropriate time for summer ascents to the Greater Ararat is the 20th June – 20th September period, while for winter ascents it is the 20th January – 20th March period.

At times, vertical and perpendicular movements typical of high mountains like the Greater Ararat, merge with general and horizontal movements of air, leading to turbulent snow storms.

Mountaineers who come across such weather during their ascents should be careful.

While "summer ascents" carried out under normal weather conditions do not present much difficulty or danger, "winter ascents" are rather difficult and dangerous, because of extreme ice formation and the risk of slipping.[4]

Name of the Station: Iğdır
Altitude: 858 m.

	I	II	III	IV	V	VI	VII	VIII	IX	X	XI	XII	Yıl
Average monthly temperature (C°)	-3	-1	6	12	17	21	24	23	19	12	6	-1	11
Sunny and partially sunny days/month	21	21	21	22	26	29	30	31	29	27	13	19	299
Average number of snow-covered days/month	14	10	2	-	-	-	-	-	-	-	1	7	33
Greatest thickness of snow-cover (cm.)	31	28	13	1	-	-	-	-	-	-	11	15	31
Average monthly relative humidity	71	66	60	59	58	55	53	54	60	68	73	76	62

Source: Bulletin of the State General Directorate of Meteorological Affairs.

The Greater Ararat and Noah's Flood

Noah's Flood, which has been described in holy texts like the Old Testament, the Bible and the Qur'an, is present also in the Sumerian-Babylonian "Epic of Gilgamesh" of around 5000 BC.

As far as we can tell from what is written in the sacred texts, God decided to renew humanity, which had acquired bad habits and could not be reformed, and having resolved to send a flood for this purpose, told Noah about this decision of His and instructed him to build an ark. Following long, careful and patient labour, Noah built a three-decker ark with a width of 22 metres, a height of 150 metres, and began to wait for the day of the flood. Finally, the flood began with very heavy rain and the present day Middle East was submerged. Noah took with him his wife, his three sons (Shem, Ham and Japheth), the wives of his sons, and two of every sort of animal, one male and one female, and thus it was that Noah survived the flood on his ark.

---

4 The first summer ascent of the Greater Ararat was carried out in July 1829 by A. von Parrot, while the first winter ascent was done on 21st February 1970 by Dr. Bozkurt Ergör. As for the first ascent and descent on skis by Turks, it took place in August 1973, as part of the celebrations of the 50th Anniversary of the Foundation of the Republic.

During the flood, Noah sailed on the waters for months, and when the waters subsided, his ark came to rest on the 2114 m. High Cudi Mountain (in Mardin - Cizre) according to the Muslim faith, or on the north-western or western slopes of the Greater Ararat (5137 m.) according to the Christian faith, after which humans began to reproduce once more and spread throughout the world. It is also claimed that the Eram Garden, where Adam and Eve lived, was located on the northern slopes of Greater Ararat (the Plain of Iğdır-Erivan).

During the last fifty years there have been many publications about Noah's Ark, with the result that a lot of attention has been paid to the Greater Ararat. However, none of the research conducted has turned out concrete results. During the decade of 1950-1960, the Frenchman F. Navara went to great lengths to find Noah's Ark, conducting research nearly every year on the western and north-western faces of the Greater Ararat. After 1960, the Americans began taking an increasingly keen interest in the subject.

When the research about Noah's Ark carried out in the 1960s by the American John Libby also failed to result in any concrete conclusions, interest in the subject subsided for some time. However, when the American astronaut James Irwin took an interest in the subject in 1981, Noah's Ark and the Greater Ararat were reintroduced as subjects considered important and interesting by world opinion.

EXCURSIONS AND ASCENTS

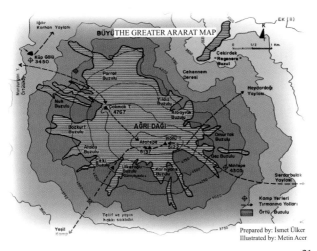

Prepared by: İsmet Ülker
Illustrated by: Metin Acer

The Greater Ararat, which is the highest peak of the Anatolian Peninsula and of Europe, attracts the attention of mountaineers throughout the world. The routes of ascent up the Greater Ararat have been indicated on the map.

The Greater Ararat with its 5137 metre height, and geological and morphological structure, is a mountain with distinguishing characteristics. The Greater Ararat, which is higher than its surrounding area and has a majestic look, is 4300 metres higher than the Plain of Iğdır and 3400 metres higher than the Plain of Doğubeyazıt. The Trabzon-Erzurum-Tehran international transit highway runs along the western and southern slopes of Ararat and proceeds into Iran. Doğubeyazıt and Iğdır, which are the towns closest to the mountain, are on this highway. The distance between Doğubeyazıt and Erzurum is 270 km., while the distance between Doğubeyazıt and the border of Iran is 33 km., with both sections being asphalted. In addition to this there are also regular air and bus connections between Ankara, Erzurum, Ağrı and Iğdır.

Ascent along the Southern Side

The most comfortable and secure ascents to the summit of Ararat are those conducted on the southern side. This side offers more favourable conditions in terms of the march and ascent, communications, transport and security. (However, local authorities have to be notified and a permit obtained from them before the ascent.)

Preparations for the ascent are done in Doğubeyazıt, a town which offers ample lodging facilities and restaurants. The teams that have to climb the mountain can leave their private belongings in these hotels, and park their cars in the parking lots of them. The mountain trek begins at Eliköy.

Eliköy can be reached from Doğubeyazıt via the Topçatan (Ganikor) Village by vehicles. The Doğubeyazıt-Topçatan road is a 7 km. long road of good quality. The approximately 8 km.-long Topçatan-Eliköy road, however, is considerably rougher. After Eliköy, equipment is carried on horse-back. After having traversed the İbrahim Kara Plateau, one reaches the first campsite, which is located an altitude of 3200. The aforementioned beasts of burden can be obtained at the village of Topçatan. The distance between Eliköy and the first campsite known as "Yeşilkamp" is 5-6 hours on foot. Mountaineers get their water at Doğubeyazıt or at the village of Topçatan. Sometimes it is possible to reach the first camp site of "Yeşilkamp" by means of cars or pickups via the village of Örtülü.

The mountaineers will generally rest for a night at the site of the first camp. The following day they will reach the second camp site at an altitude of 4000 metres.

Part of the camp equipment will be carried on horse-back up to an altitude of 3500 metres. There is a distance of 3-4 hours between the first camp and the second camp. At the second camp site there is a constant flow of water resulting from melting ice or snow.

In general, it is from this camp site that mountaineers begin their ascent to the peak. The ridge leading from the campsite towards the peak is the normal route of ascent. Mountaineers who have begun their ascent from the second campsite will in normal circumstances reach Mount Ararat's summit in 7-8 hours. Mountaineers beginning their ascent at the first campsite on the other hand will take 10-12 hours to reach the mountain's summit. It is obligatory for mountaineers climbing to the summit of Ararat to have with them ice heel irons, ice pickaxes and rope. The ascent should not be attempted unless the previous night has been clear and starry. Summer ascents of the Greater Ararat are not very difficult. Winter ascents, one the other hand, are very difficult and dangerous. Due to extreme icing and the risk of slipping, the ridge between the altitudes of 4850 and 4950 metres should be climbed using ropes and security precautions.

Ascent along the Eastern Side

For the ascent up the Greater Ararat along its eastern side, the Serdarbulak Plateau is reached over Iğdır and Aralık's county seat. The Serdarbulak Plateau located at an altitude of 2600 metres between the Greater and the Lesser Ararat can be reached by means of normal vehicles.

This is where the first camp will be set up. Later, the location at 4300 metres called Mıhtepe will be reached with backpacks and there the second camp will be established.

The ascent to the summit will begin at Mıhtepe. Under normal weather conditions, reaching the summit from there and returning to the camp will last 6-8 hours.

Ascent along the North-western Side: "The Parrot Route"

For the ascent along this route, mountaineers will first go by car from Iğdır to the Korhan Plateau (2000 m.). The first 10 km. of the road are asphalt, while the last 16 km. are pressed earth. The first camp will be set up on the Korhan Plateau on the north side of the mountain. At that location there is a mountain and ski refuge and a post of the gendarmerie. After having rested for a day there, the Küp Gölü Lake at an altitude of 3450 metres will be reached on the second day. The mountaineers, who will have set up camp at the Küp Gölü, will ascend to the peak from there along the "Parrot Route" and will return to the camp the same day. This ascent along the Parrot Glacier will last around 8-10 hours.

It is also possible to begin from Karaağaç on the Iğdır-Doğubeyazıt highway rather than from this camp. Mountain and nature lovers, on tractors or on foot, will first reach the "Monzurgan (Mozurgan)" Plateau (2750 m.). From there they can reach Küp Gölü, and then after having set up camp there, they can ascend to the peak over the Parrot Glacier.

Excursion and Ascent Programme

A) Ascent along the Southern Slope:

1st day: Doğubeyazıt-Topçatan V., Eliköy, Yeşilkamp (3200 m.)

2nd day: Rest at Yeşilkamp.

3rd day: Yeşilkamp 2nd camp site (4000 m.)

4th day: Ascent to the summit (5137 m.)

B) Ascent along the North-western Slope Yamaçtan:

1st day: Iğdır-Korhan Plateau (2000 m.)

2nd day: Korhan Plateau - Küp Gölü (3450 m.)

3rd day: Rest at the camp site

4th day: Ascent to the peak

C) Ascent along the Eastern Slope:

1st day: Iğdır-Aralık-Serdarbulak (2600 m.)

2nd day: Serdarbulak-Mıhtepe (4300 m.)

3rd day: Rest at Mıhtepe

4th day: Ascent to the peak

Mountaineers wishing to climb the Greater Ararat, either in summer or in winter, are required to have ice pickaxes and ropes for mountaineering. As for mountaineers wishing to climb in the winter, they should have also ice grapples, a carbine and snow goggles.

Updated Information and Warnings

Ascents to the Greater Ararat (5137 m.) are subject to the authorisation of the Office of the Governor of Ağrı. People in Turkey wishing to carry out the ascent will apply directly for a permit to the Office of the Governor of Ağrı, while those from foreign countries must apply via an embassy or consulate in their own country. Ascents have to be carried out under the supervision of official guides. There has to be one official guide for every five people. Each mountaineer will pay a 50 dollar fee for the ascent.

Teams wishing to climb in the winter are required to have undergone training in "secure climbing" over icy surfaces, and in the use of ice pickaxes, ice heel irons and ice grapples. It should be kept in mind that especially while going over the "ice cap glacier" ridge at an altitude of 4850-4950 m., the normal route of ascent should be maintained and "secure passage by rope" should be carried out. Whenever there are strong horizontal or vertical air movements or precipitations, the ascent to the peak should be interrupted, and the team should wait in a state of resting.

Mountaineers climbing the Greater Ararat should have sleeping bags, inflatable mattresses and mountain tents with them. There are no lodging facilities like mountain refuges or mountain cottages along the routes of ascent on the Greater Ararat.

It is not advisable to carry out solitary and unguided ascents to the peak of Ararat. Mountaineers wishing to carry out a winter ascent should have the necessary experience and equipment. Because of extreme icing and the consequent risk of slipping, "winter ascents" of the Greater Ararat should always be approached with great care.

Teams ascending along the north-western or western routes should when necessary set up a second camp on the Parrot Glacier and, having ascended the peak from there, should return to camp on the same day.

Mountaineers ascending the Greater Ararat in the summer should be equipped against the rays of the sun, should have sunglasses, light-coloured hats with wide brims, and should wear light coloured cotton or woollen clothes. Everyone who visits Ararat, for whatever reason, should not forget to go to Örtülüköy to buy various kinds of carpets and to visit İshakpaşa Palace on their way back.

For Further Details:

General Directorate for Youth and Sports
Turkish Mountaineering Federation
4th Floor Ulus / ANKARA
Phone: 0(312) 311 91 20 - Fax: 0(312) 310 15 78
Website: www.tdf.org.tr

Office of the Governor of Ağrı, AĞRI
Phone: 0(472) 215 37 30 - Fax: 0(472) 215 39 18
Website: agri.kulturturizm.gov.tr

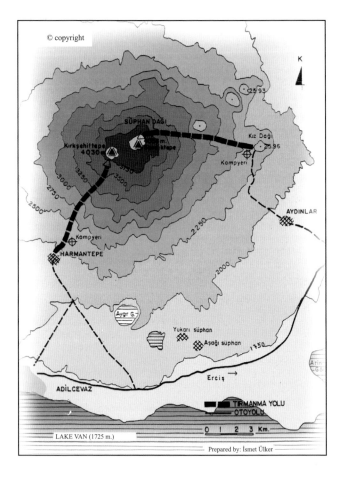

© copyright

SÜPHAN DAĞI

Kırkşehiftepe
4030 m.

Kız Dağı
2593

Kampyeri

AYDINLAR

Kampyeri

HARMANTEPE

Aygır G.

Yukarı süphan

Aşağı süphan

Erciş →

ADİLCEVAZ

TIRMANMA YOLU
OTOYOLU

0 1 2 3 Km.

LAKE VAN (1725 m.)

Prepared by: İsmet Ülker

MOUNT SÜPHAN (4058 m.)

Mount Süphan is the third highest mountain after the Greater Ararat and Uludoruk "Reşko". Mount Süphan (4058 m.) rises amongst the chain of volcanoes in eastern Anatolia, or, to be more precise, the Süphan Volcano is located at the centre of this chain, which constitutes an "orographic" border between the Lake Van and the Upper Murat basins. At the northernmost tip of the chain of volcanoes in eastern Anatolia, which extends in the direction of SW-NE, lies the Greater Ararat (5137 m.).

To the south of the Süphan Volcano, the slopes of which begin to rise from the western coast of Lake Van, are the Adilcevaz and Ahlat county seats, while to its north are the Erciş and Patnos county seats. In other words, Mount Süphan is located within the borders of the provinces of Bitlis, Van and Ağrı, and at the junction of the borders of these three provinces. However, the greatest part of the mountain lies in the province of Bitlis.

Geological Structure and Geomorphology

Mount Süphan is a 4058 m. high volcano formed by volcanic activities that began at the end of the second half (Neogene) of the Tertiary Period and continued throughout the Quaternary Period.

Mount Süphan is a cluster volcano consisting of a main volcano and many secondary conduits ending in smaller craters and volcanic cones. However, the mountain itself was formed by means of a central eruption through a single main conduit.

Mount Süphan, which occupies an area with a diameter of around 24 km., has two summits. These are Sandıktepe (4058 m.) on the north-eastern part of the mountain and Kırkşehit Tepe (4030 m.) on its western part. At the summit of Mount Süphan is a crater, measuring around 750 m. in diameter, which has been damaged by external forces.

Sandıktepe is a "parasitical volcano" formed during the last stage of volcanic activities on Mount Süphan, and is located on the north-eastern part of the crater. A "valley glacier" lies within the crater extending along an east-west axis. The crater bottom is at an altitude of 3750 metres.

Mount Süphan was formed by a central eruption through a main crater and consists of layers of lava measuring thousands of metres, and as such is a "strato volcano". The lower parts are dominated by volcanic tuff and basaltic lava. The parts at an altitude of 2250-2500 metres consist of pink andesite, while higher parts consist of volcanic erupted stones of dark blue andesite and dasite. (Dr. Türkünal, 1980)

Layers of lava formed of andesite, dasite and other similar stones of an acidic nature that cool off rapidly have made it possible for Mount Süphan to reach its present day altitude (4058 m.). However, on Mount Süphan there are also parasitical volcanic cones and secondary conduit volcanic craters. Kızdağı (2596 m.), which is a parasitical cone, and the Aygır Lake (1942 m.), which is a secondary conduit crater lake, are two examples.

Formations of Glaciers on Mount Süphan

The summit of Mount Süphan is located above the permanent snow line, which in the case of Mount Süphan is 3600 metres. Mount Süphan was subject to greater glacial activity during the Quaternary "Diluvial" Period, and today one finds on it glaciers of both the present and fossil kinds.

On the summit of Mount Süphan is the glacier "Kırklar Lake," located at the bottom of the existing crater at an altitude of 3650 metres, and a valley glacier located at an altitude of 3750-3400 metres. This valley glacier, which has a length of around 1.5 km. and a width of 300-400 metres, extends from the bottom of the crater towards the north-east. There are fossils of glaciers like "glacial abrasions" on the north side of the mountain at an altitude of 3200 metres, and on the southern slopes at an altitude of 3375 metres.

Hydrology, flora and fauna

Mount Süphan, which rises above the western coast of Lake Van and receives heavy snowfall in the winters, serves as a kind of water depot for its surrounding area. It does so by regularly feeding underground streams thanks to the melting of glaciers and frozen snow in the summer.

The water resulting from the melting of snow and ice quickly begins to flow freely and then to permeate porous formations, thus proceeding down to lower layers. Surface water that flows according to gravity and inclination forms a kind of underground "unconfined aquifer". In general, such water surfaces at the junction of volcanic and sedimentary areas at the base and in other places near the level of Lake Van, as abundant water sources.

It is for this reason that there are not many lakes or streams on the higher parts of Mount Süphan, apart from the main crater or secondary conduit crater lakes.

Rising from the coast of Lake Van, Mount Süphan is a mountain devoid of forests. Those parts of the mountain located above an altitude of 2000 metres are almost completely covered by pastures and Alpine meadows.

The most common wild animals on Mount Süphan are wolves and bears. Among the birds found on the mountain is the Caspian Snowcock (Tetraogallus Caspius). As for reptiles, one may encounter snakes.

Climatic Conditions and Climbing Seasons

On Mount Süphan, which is located on the western part of the Lake Van Basin, and in its surrounding area, there is a continental climate of a partially "temperate" nature. The meteorological station closest to Mount Süphan, where summers are dry and hot, and winters cold with considerable snowfall, is located at Ahlat. The climatic data obtainded from this station is provided in the following table. One should keep in mind that on those parts of Mount Süphan located at an altitude of over 3000 metres there is a mountain climate of extremely cold air at night and strong heat during the day.

In the case of Mount Süphan, where there are horizontal and vertical atmospheric movements, spring and autumn ascents are not recommended. The most appropriate time for summer ascents is the 20th June - 20th September period, while for winter ascents it is the 20th January - 20th March period. In the case of winter ascents, climbers are recommended to set up two camps, one at 2500 metres and the other at 3500 metres, and to carry out the ascent as a team.

Name of the station: Ahlat
Altitude: 1750 m.

	I	II	III	IV	V	VI	VII	VIII	IX	X	XI	XII	Yıl
Average monthly temperature (C°)	-2	-2	8	7	13	18	22	22	17	10	5	1	9
Sunny and partially sunny days/ month	18	17	20	21	26	29	31	31	29	28	25	21	297
Average number of snow-covered days/month	19	23	18	3	-	-	-	-	-	-	1	11	74
Greatest thickness of snow-cover (cm.)	129	107	70	20	5	-	-	-	-	-	45	50	129
Average monthly relative humidity	77	71	72	71	63	58	59	56	59	72	80	73	68

Source: Bulletin of the State General Directorate of Meteorological Affairs

EXCURSIONS AND ASCENTS

Mount Süphan is an extinct volcano characterised by a gradually rising topography. It is for this reason that climbing this mountain does not present technical difficulties (save for the height). It is possible to climb Mount Süphan (4058 m.) and reach its summit by means of mountain treks of medium difficulty, from all sides.

However, in terms of both accessibility and ease of climbing as well as with respect to the views seen during the ascent, the eastern and western slopes of Mount Süphan are more attractive and suitable for excursions and climbings.

Climbing Mount Süphan Along the Eastern Slope

To ascent Mount Süphan along its eastern slope, you first have to go to the village of Aydınlar on the western side of the Adilcevaz-Erciş highway. You then proceed to the village of Kıçgılı by car, and from there climb to Kızdağı. If necessary, you can get a mountain guide at Kıçgılı. The distance between Adilcevaz and Aydınlar, which consists of a tarmac road, is around 25 km., while the distance between Aydınlar and Kızdağı is 10 km. The ascent to Mount Süphan begins from Kızdağı (2596 m.). Following a trek of 6-7 hours you reach Sandıktepe (4058 m.), which is the highest point of Mount Süphan and is situated to the north-east of the crater. Mountaineers carry their food and water with them. After having passed the crater and the mountain glacier, which has a length of around 1.5 km., you return to Kızdağı along the same route. The return trip lasts about 3-4 hours.

Climbing Mount Süphan Along the Southern Slope

Those wishing to ascend Mount Süphan along its southern slope first have to go to the Adilcevaz county seat to the south of the mountain. From there you proceed to the village of Harmantepe (Norşincik) by car. Harmantepe, which is located at an altitude of around 2200 m., is connected to Adilcevaz by means of a 10 km.-long, normal road of stabilised earth.

Excursions to Mount Süphan and ascents to its summit begin at the village of Harmantepe. After a normal trek and ascent lasting around 7-8 hours, Kırkşehit Peak (4030 m.), which is the mountain's second highest peak, is reached. During this excursion and ascent, it is possible to see the crater at the summit of Mount Süphan, the parasitical volcanic cones in this crater, the Mount Süphan Glacier at the bottom of the crater, and various crater lakes, after which the descent begins. Following the same route as that used for the ascent, return is made to the village of Harmantepe. The return trip lasts around 4-5 hours.

Winter Sports

On the 4058 metre-high Mount Süphan, there is snowfall all winter long. Snow accumulation can reach heights of up to 2-3 metres. Mount Süphan not only provides an environment suitable for winter sports in terms of the thickness of snow cover and the incline of the mountain, but it also offers the possibilities of high mountain excursions on skis or "Heliski" skiing, which is high altitude skiing done via helicopter.

Use of lodging facilities like the hotels or motels in Ahlat or Tatvan is possible while taking part in sports activities, both in summer and winter.

Routes for summer ascents are recommended for winter ascents to the summit of Mount Süphan as well. Teams carrying out a "climb on skis" should definitely keep in a straight line and within eye sight of each other during descent, and should be especially cautious in the case of the appearance of sudden fog.

Excursion and Climbing Programme

Summer Ascent along the Eastern Side
1st day: Adilcevaz-Aydınlar-Kızdağı
2nd day: Kızdağı-Mount Süphan (4058 m.)
3rd day: Kızdağı and return to Adilcevaz

Summer Ascent along the Southern Side
1st day: Adilcevaz-Harmantepe
2nd day: Harmantepe-Mount Süphan (4030 m.)
3rd day: Harmantepe and return to Adilcevaz

HAKKARİ CİLO-SAT MOUNTAINS (4136 m.)

The Taurus folded mountains, located among the Alpine-Himalayan mountain formation, penetrate Eastern Anatolia in the form of three branches: the North-eastern Tauruses, the Central Tauruses and the South-eastern Tauruses. The beginning of the South-eastern Tauruses consists of the Amanos Mountains and the continuation of the Nurhak Mountains. This mountain chain, which extends to Hakkari along the south of Maraş, Malatya, Elazığ, Muş and Bitlis, reaches the mountainous area of Southern Iran.

The South-eastern Tauruses reach heights of 2600 m. to the south of Malatya, 2350 m. in Elazığ and 2700 m. around Muş and Bitlis, where they spread over a rather large area, before growing narrower and gaining in height beginning just south of Lake Van. The South-eastern Tauruses, which reach a height of 3400-3600 metres to the south of Lake Van, rise to an altitude of over 4000 metres once within the boundaries of the province of Hakkari. As we have already mentioned briefly, the Cilo-Sat Mountains, which are located on the "Alpine-Himalayan" mountain formation and which make up part of the Tauruses, are within the boundaries of the province of Hakkari.

These winding mountains, which in general extend along an east-west axis, cover an area measuring around 50 km. in length and 30 km. in width, and consist of two parts. The part bordered by the Zab River to the west, by the Oramar Çayı stream to the east, and by the Nehil Çayı stream to the north is called the "Cilo Mountains". To the east of the Cilo Mountains rise the Sat Mountains. To the north of the Sat Mountains lies the city of Yüksekova, and to their south the village Dağlıca (Oramar).

Uludoruk "Reşko" (4136 m.), Erinç Tepe "Glacier Mountain" (4116 m.), Bobek Tepe (3980 m.) and Poyraz Tepe (3900 m.) are the highest peaks of these mountains. All in all, the Sat Mountains are lower than the Cilo Mountains. The highest of peak of the latter chain is Mount Çatalkaya "Samdi" (3794 m.).

The Earliest Studies Concerning the Cilo-Sat Mountains

The first scientific study of the Cilo-Sat Mountains was carried out in 1937 by Dr. Hans Bobek from Berlin University. Dr. H. Bobek was accompanied by 5 mountaineers and scientists from the Innsbruck Mountaineering Club. The results of these studies led by Dr. Bobek were published in 1938 (Petermanns Mitteilungen 1938, Haft Mai, Berlin).

In 1944, the Turkish Mountaineering and Winter Sports Federation organised a special mountaineering and study programme encompassing the Cilo-Sat Mountains. Dr. Reşat İzbırak from the Physical Geography Department of the Languages, History and Geography Faculty of Ankara University took part in this mission. In 1947, Dr. Süleyman Türkünal began to carry out the first geological studies of the Cilo-Sat Mountains.

In 1948, the Turkish Mountaineering and Winter Sports Federation organised a second expedition to the Cilo-Sat Mountains, in which Dr. Sırrı Erinç from the Geography Department of Istanbul University took part.

After 1960, missions to and studies of the Cilo-Sat Mountains began to increase in number and intensity. Two mountaineering and study commissions to the Cilo-Sat Mountains, led by this book's writer Geomorphologist-Geologist İsmet Ülker, were carried out in 1962 and in 1965. During these expeditions and ascents, the Glacier Morphology of the Cilo and Sat Mountains was studied and a seminar thesis on the topic was prepared.

Geological Structure and Topography

According to the study briefly mentioned above, the Cilo-Sat Mountains are located on a tectonic unit of the Alpine-Himalayan mountain formation called "Iranid". According to the observations of Dr. Geologist Süleyman Türkünal, the basis of the Cilo-Sat Mountains consists of a winding and broken "peneplain" of the Paleozoic era. Above this basis formed of crystalline schists there are sedimentary series of the Mesozoic and Tertiary periods with internal eruption layers.

The highest parts of the Cilo-Sat Mountains are in general made up of massive and crystalline limestone containing ophiolite (volcanic green sections). As for the higher parts of the Sat Mountains, they consist solely of intermediary and nucleus eruption ophiolites and granites. The series of layers making up the Cilo Mountains, which have a length of around 50 km. and a width of 30 km., have in general a NW inclination. The Cilo Mountains were eroded towards the end of the Miocene Epoch Tertiary Period, becoming a "peneplain", after which they rose once more and, having been folded, began to erode.

The higher parts of the Cilo and Sat Mountains were eroded by glaciers during the "Diluvial" era of the Quaternary Period, and by both glaciers and rivers during the "Fluvial" era, with the result that they fragmented and changed shape to acquire their present-day rough and forbidding aspect. This strong erosion continues today. The Cilo Mountains, which 2000 m. to the south of Yüksekova reach an altitude of 4136 m., consist of three belts with respect to their geological structure and topography.

The Tertiary Series to the North

These series from the Tertiary Period, which are made up of limestone, limestone with marl and sandstone in some places, are located between Yüksekova and Gelyano Lake and have the morphological look of a "plateau". These series from the Tertiary Period give rise to thick exposures to the south of Gelyano Lake and on the northern slopes of the Beyazsu "Avaspi" Valley, leading to a structure with "layered steps".

The Upper-Cretaceous High Summits Belt

This belt, encompassing the high peaks of the Cilo Mountains, is made up of grey, hard and massive crystalline limestone containing radiolarite and (volcanic green mass) ophiolite series. The highest peaks of the Cilo Mountains are to be found in this belt, which has an altitude of over 4000 metres, such as in the cases of Uludoruk "Reşko" (4136 m.) or Erinç Tepe (4116 m.)

The Trias Belt with Steps in the South

This belt making up the southern part of the Cilo Mountains consists of limestone series with black marl intermediate layers. Above this series there are limestone series of the Cretaceous era, with a thickness of 1500-2000 metres. These geological layers make up the "Southern Cilo Layered Steps Area".

The plain of Yüksekova "Gevar", which lies to the north of the Sat Mountains at an altitude of 2000 metres above sea level, is a tectonic subsidence area, to the south of which is an active fault line.

Glacier Morphology in the Cilo-Sat Mountains

It is in the area of the Cilo-Sat Mountains that glacier topography, and consequently glacier erosion and sedimentation, are at their strongest in Turkey. With respect to its general appearance and glacier topography, this area is similar to the Alps.

The İzbırak Glacier, the "Eastern Reşko Glacier" and the Erinç Glacier on the Cilo-Sat Mountains, and the Çatalkaya Glacier on the Sat Mountains, are the main glaciers. The biggest glacier of the Cilo Mountains is the İzbırak Glacier. This glacier is embedded at an altitude of 3500 m.-3150 m., has a length of around 5 km., a width of 500-600 m. and in places is as thick as 30-40 metres. The İzbırak Glacier, which is embedded in a deep glacier valley, has

crevasses running along its width in the narrower parts of the valley, and crevasses running along its length in the larger parts. At the end of the glacier there is an active glacier "moraine" barrier. As for the Erinç Glacier, it is located between the 3500-3100 metre altitudes and has similar characteristics.[5]

The biggest glacier on the Sat Mountains is embedded in the Sat-Gevaruk Valley. A branch of this glacier, which has a length of around 3 km., extends into the Bay Lake. The glaciers on the Cilo-Sat Mountains are mostly situated at the 2900-3500 metre altitude belt. There are 10 glaciers in this area. During the Diluvial Ice Age there were even more glaciers in the Cilo-Sat Mountainous Area than there are today. For example, on the NE and NW slopes of Uludoruk "Reşko" are two big, ancient glacier valleys. The "Eastern Reşko" ancient glacier valley, with a length of 10 km., is embedded at the 1900-3500 metre altitude belt. The "Beyazsu Valley", a similar ancient glacier valley of the same dimension, is located on the north-west of Uludoruk.

---

5 Prof. Dr. Reşat İZBIRAK and Prof. Dr. Sırrı ERİNÇ are the first specialists of physical geography to have carried out scientific studies in this area in 1944 and in 1948.

The Sat Mountains rising to the east of the Cilo Mountains, and to the south of Yüksekova, have a different structure from that of the Cilo Mountains, with respect to geological structure and of the topography. The Sat Mountains have the look of a high mountain area formed by the eruption of stones that constitute the nucleus of the crumpled mountain chain. The Sat Mountains, which in places are made of sedimentary rocks of limestone or of similar materials, have been subjected to strong fluvial and glacial erosion.

On the Sat Mountains there are many glacier lakes and mountain glaciers that are still active today. The primary glacier lakes are Satbaşı lakes, and the lakes of Gevaruk and Bay. As for the mountain and valley glaciers, they are mostly embedded on the northern slopes of the Gevaruk and Çatalkaya peaks. Those parts of the Sat Mountains located at altitudes of over 2500 metres possess a rough and forbidding topography, and also witness heavy frozen snowfall and glacier erosion.

In conclusion:

-Presently there is intense glacier erosion taking place in those parts of the Cilo-Sat Mountains with altitudes of more than 2900 metres.

-In the altitudes between 1900-2900 metres there is erosion by glaciers, frozen snow and also by streams, while at altitudes lower than 1900 metres one finds only fluvial erosion and the consequent morphology.

Streams and Lakes "Hydrology"

The Great Zab River, which flows through the western part of the Hakkari-Cilo Mountains extending in the NW-SE direction, cuts through these mountains through a deep "gorge" running in the NS direction. The average altitude of this area is 3500 metres, while the floor of the valley of the Great Zab, which is the biggest river of the area, has an altitude of 1310 m. at the Beyazsu conjunction. The main tributaries of the Great Zab, which has an average valley depth of 2000-2500 metres, are the Nehil Çayı collecting the water of Yüksekova and of its surrounding mountains and the Beyazsu "Avaspi" stream collecting the water of the glaciers to the west of Uludoruk (Reşko).

Another tributary of the Great Zab is the Avarobaşin Stream that runs between the Cilo and the Sat Mountains. This stream collects the water of the glaciers and the frozen water of Doğu Reşko and of the Sat Mountains.

There are many glacier lakes also on the Cilo and Sat Mountains. However, the Sat Mountains are richer in lakes, because of their soil, which in parts is not permeable. The biggest lake on the Cilo Mountains is the Gelyano Lake, which is located at an altitude of 2950 metres. This lake, which measures around 300 metres in diameter, is an ancient glacier "cirque" lake.

The main glacier lakes, which are more frequent on the Sat Mountains, are the Satbaşı, Gevaruk and Bay Lakes. Of these, the Bay Lake at an altitude of 2870 m., is particularly important because of its dimension and altitude. On the slopes rising above the south-western side of this lake, which has a length of 3 km. along a N-S axis, there are four valley glaciers. These glaciers and lakes have been indicated in the relevant maps.

Natural Vegetation and Wildlife "Flora and fauna"

Even though a large part of the Cilo and Sat Mountains lies within forest boundaries, the mountains themselves possess little in the way of forests.

The higher parts of the area are rocky and barren. Within the area as a whole, the only parts where oak trees (Guercus sp.) and pine trees are dense enough to form forests, are the bottoms of low valleys and the southern slopes of mountains. In the deep valley bottoms, which possess a temperate climate, walnuts and fruit are grown and vineyards are cultivated.

The entirety of the area (except the bottoms of low valleys) lies within the Alpine meadow belt. Alpine meadows are common at altitudes of 2000-3100 metres, but are replaced by year-round snow, frozen snow and glaciers at higher altitudes.

Bears are the most common wild animals on the Cilo-Sat Mountains. Mountaineers and those on research excursions to the area frequently encounter innocuous families of bears. Wolves are among other wild animal species living in the area. In addition, local people claim to have sighted a kind of panther on the southern slopes of the Cilo Mountains from time to time.

Climatic Conditions and Climbing Seasons

To the south of the Cilo-Sat Mountains there are vast, arid steppes. This notwithstanding, the Cilo and Sat Mountains receive plenty of rain due to their height. The rainy season is winter. As a result of the high altitude, precipitation takes the form of snowfall. It is for this reason that the glacier topography in the area is complex and varied. The bottoms of deep valleys have a more temperate climate (a microclimate). These valley bottoms, where vineyard and orchards may exist, provide the most suitable environment for rural settlements. True enough, all the villages on the Cilo-Sat Mountains are located on these valley bottoms. Some of the climatic data from the meteorological stations of Hakkari and Yüksekova for this area, which in the summer is dry and cool, have been indicated in the following tables. The most suitable time for summer ascents to the Cilo and Sat Mountains are the months of June, July and August, while for winter ascents the best period is that of 20th January - 20th March.

Name of the Station: Hakkari
Altitude: 1720 m.

	I	II	III	IV	V	VI	VII	VIII	IX	X	XI	XII	Yıl
Average monthly temperature (C°)	-5	-4	2	7	14	20	24	24	19	12	6	-2	10
Sunny and partially sunny days/month	21	19	22	22	26	30	31	31	30	28	25	21	305
Average number of snow-covered days/month	28	28	23	4	-	-	-	-	-	-	2	18	103
Greatest thickness of snow-cover (cm.)	206	204	134	134	-	-	-	-	-	7	40	10	217
Average monthly relative humidity	72	73	69	64	53	41	39	38	41	55	64	74	57

Source: Bulletin of the State General Directorate of Meteorological Affairs

Name of the Station: Yüksekova
Altitude: 1900 m.

	I	II	III	IV	V	VI	VII	VIII	IX	X	XI	XII	Yıl
Average monthly temperature (C°)	-9	-10	-1	5	12	17	20	21	15	9	4	-6	6
Sunny and partially sunny days/month	19	19	21	23	29	30	31	31	30	26	27	21	306
Average number of snow-covered days/month	31	28	30	11	-	-	-	-	-	-	5	25	130
Greatest thickness of snow-cover (cm.)	175	215	200	114	5	-	-	-	-	9	22	140	215
Average monthly relative humidity	80	80	79	71	59	51	50	50	50	68	70	80	66

Source: Bulletin of the State General Directorate of Meteorological Affairs

The most suitable time for summer excursions and ascents to the Hakkari Cilo-Sat Mountains consists of the months of June, July, August and September. However, by September the natural environment loses some of its richness. As for winter ascents, the most suitable time consists of the months of February and March. On the other hand, there is the danger of avalanches in November, December and January because of fresh and not yet settled snow, and in April and May because of melting below the surface, wetness and slippage. It is for this reason that the months of February and March are recommended for winter ascents.

EXCURSIONS AND ASCENTS

As it has already been mentioned, the Cilo-Sat Mountains, which are a continuation of the South-eastern Taurus folded mountains, rise within the borders of the province of Hakkari. This chain of mountains extending along the SW-NE axis consists of two parts: the Cilo Mountains and the Sat Mountains.

It is not known who was the first to complete a summer ascension to Uludoruk "Reşko" (4136 m.), which is the highest peak of the Cilo-Sat Mountains. However, the first winter ascent to this peak was carried out on 5th March 1982 by two Turkish mountaineers, Muzaffer Özdemir from Ankara and Kemal Çapa from Yüksekova.

People wanting to carry out excursions and ascents on these mountains will first have to go to Hakkari via Van. The city of Van has regular highway and rail connections to Ankara via Erzurum and Elazığ. In addition to this, there are also regular flights between Van and Ankara. The city of Van, which is set on the shores of the eponymous lake, offers a sufficient number of quality lodging facilities possessing touristic licences.

People wishing to carry out excursions or ascents to the Cilo-Sat Mountains will complete their final preparations in Van, and from there go either to Hakkari or to Yüksekova. The distance between Van and Hakkari is 245 km. Most of the road is paved with asphalt. The distance between Van and Yüksekova is 260 km., and the road in this case is entirely paved with asphalt. Those wishing to carry out excursions or ascents on the Cilo Mountains will begin their trek at the village of Serpil or via the Hakkari-Beyazsu Valley. Those traversing the Beyazsu Valley will either climb on foot or be transported by vehicles to the Beyazsu "Mergan" Plateau to the west of Uludoruk (4136 m.). Expeditions to the Sat Mountains will begin at the village of Yeşiltaş (İştazın), which is across from the village of Serpil, or from İkiyaka, the village Sat Köyü, further to the south.

Entrance to the Cilo Mountains from the West
"The Beyazsu Valley Route"

This valley is located at a distance of 18 km. from Hakkari, on the main highway and across from the Zap gendarmerie post. Mountaineers who embark on their expedition from the Zap gendarmerie post on foot or by vehicle will first go to the village of Dez and from there once more on foot or by vehicle will reach their first campsite. On foot, the distance between the gendarmerie post and the first camp site will be covered in 6-8 hours. The camp site is the Beyazsu "Mergan" Plateau. Its altitude is 2550 m. Mountaineers who have set up camp on the Beyazsu Plateau will carry out reconaissance tours, so as to be able to choose the route that best suits their own personal capabilities. It is possible while staying at this camp to carry out special, hihgly difficult ascents to peaks like Uludoruk (Reşko) 4136 m. or Erinçtepe (Glacier Mountain) 4116 m.

There are high mountain glaciers around the campsite, such as the Western Reşko Glacier to its south, and the Erinç Glacier to its south-west. Mountaineers will proceed through the "Der-i Cafer Passage" on the Mergan Plateau, and then via the Orişa Yurdu-Gelyano Lake and "Der-i Kervan" passage reach the Serpil Plateau. The distance between the Mergan Plateau and Orişa Yurdu is four hours, while the distance between Orişa Yurdu and Serpil Plateau is around six hours. It is also possible, when on Mergan Plateau to go through the "Deri Kün Passage" and by means of a natural ascent reach the Eastern Reşko Valley. However, during this passage it will not be possible to use pack animals.

Ascent to Uludoruk (Reşko) (4136 m.)

Normal ascents to the "Reşko" or "Gelyaşin" peak, which in new maps is called Uludoruk, are done via the Serpil Plateau. Gelyaşin means "Blue Fort". There are various routes for the ascent to Uludoruk or "Reşko Peak". Mountaineers can find their own routes or follow the routes indicated on the relevant maps.

Ascent Route Number (I):
Camp is set up to the south of the Der'i Kervan passage, near the İzbırak (Reşko) Glacier. Mountaineers will carry out reconaissance tours before the ascent. The ascent will begin at the campsite. The Great "İzbırak Glacier" will be passed. Following the glacier, the Uludoruk "Reşko" Peak (4136 m.) will be reached by means of an ascent over rock.

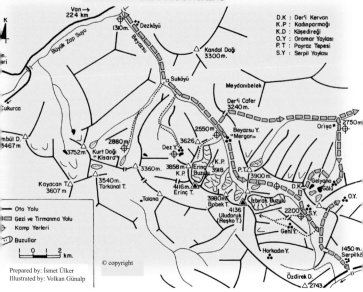

D.K : Der'i Kervan
K.P : Kadınparmağı
K.D : Köşedireği
O.Y : Oramar Yaylası
P.T : Poyraz Tepesi
S.Y : Serpil Yaylası

Prepared by: İsmet Ülker
Illustrated by: Volkan Günalp

© copyright

(Mountaineers not sufficiently competent in glacier or rock climbing should not attempt this route.)

Ascent Route Number (II):
Camp is set up on Serpil Plateau.[6] The 500 metre-high sheer cliff rising to the south of the camp will be overcome by natural and rope-aided ascent. Following the wall, the ascent will continue towards the right until Uludoruk (4136 m.) is reached. Using the same route for the return trip would present great difficulties. This is why during the return trip to the camp site on Gehi Plateau, the large valley bottom extending from west to east will be followed.[7]

Ascent Route Number (III):
This route is the easiest and safest route to Uludoruk or Reşko Peak. Those preferring this route should set up camp 3 km. below Serpil Plateau. To the west of the campsite there is a great passage "neck" over the valley slopes extending like a wall. This passage is the beginning of the shortest ascent route. Mountaineers ascending from here will reach Reşko (4136 m.) summit within 7-8 hours. The "Gehi Plateau" lies along the ascent route.

---

6 In this area, plateau (highland) settlements are called "zoma".

7 The writer of this book, İsmet ÜLKER, carried out his 2nd ascent to Uludoruk (4136 m.) in 1965 following this route. It is for this reason that this route of ascent is called "The Ülker Route".

Excursions and Ascents to the Sat Mountains

Mountaineers who have completed their excursions and ascents of the Cilo Mountains, will proceed to the Sat Mountains. The most convenient passage from the Cilo Mountains to the Sat Mountains is that via the Serpil and Yeşiltaş (1350 m.) villages. Mountaineers will climb to the Satbaşı Plateau (3000 m.) via the Yeşiltaş-Dehi Plateau. From there they will proceed to the Sat Gevaruk Plateau (2850 m.). The distance between Yeşiltaş and the Sat Gevaruk Plateau can be covered on foot in around 6-8 hours. Camp will be established at the Satbaşı Plateau or at the Sat Gevaruk Plateau. Excursions can be organised to the summits and glaciers to the south of the campsite. Mountaineers will determine themselves the routes of ascent to these peaks, which rise as high as 3794 metres.

The most suitable campsite for ascents to the peaks is the Sat-Gevaruk Plateau. Mountaineers who have completed their excursions and ascents at Sat Gevaruk will proceed to Bay Lake. The distance between Sat Gevaruk and Bay Lake is four hours. Around Bay Lake all four seasons exist at the same time. The altitude of Bay Lake is 2870 m. The high mountains and valley glaciers around Bay Lake offer a majestic view and are reflected on the surface of the lake. The camp will be set up on the north shore of the lake. Mountain and nature lovers who have completed their excursions and ascents will return from Bay Lake to Yüksekova. On foot this route will last around 10 hours.

Mountaineers wishing to enter the Sat Mountains via Yüksekova will first go to the village of Yeşiltaş using the highway. From there they will enter on foot the Sat Mountains. As for the load, it will be carried on mules, as is the case for the Cilo Mountains as well.

Excursion and Ascent Programme

1st day: Hakkari-Dez Village-Beyazsu Plateau (2550 m.).

2nd day: Camp at the Beyazsu "Mergan" Plateau.

3rd day: Erinç Glacier and ascent to the peak (4116 m.).

4th day: Excursion to Uludoruk and to the Western Reşko Glacier or ascent to Western Reşko "Uludoruk".

5th day: Beyazsu Plateau-Orişa Yurdu.

6th day: Orişa Yurdu-Gelyano Lake-Serpil Plateau.

7th day: İzbırak Glacier and area reconnaissance.

8th day: Ascent from Serpil Plateau to Uludoruk (Reşko) (4136 m.).

9th day: Serpil Village-Satbaşı Plateau.

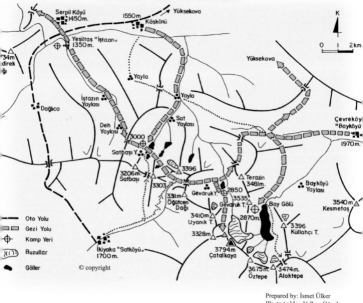

Prepared by: İsmet Ülker
Illustrated by: Volkan Günalp

10th day: Satbaşı Plateau-Satgevaruk Plateau.

11th day: Çatalkaya ascent (3794 m.).

12th day: Satgevaruk-Bay Lake.

13th day: Camp at Bay Lake.

14th day: Ascent to the peak.

15th day: Bay Lake –Yüksekova.

Updated Information and Recommendations

The Cilo and Sat Mountains are closed to excursions and ascents because of security reasons. It is only with special permission from the Hakkari Governor's Office that excursions and ascents can be carried out in this area.

The most suitable entry points to the Cilo Mountains are Beyazsu and the village of Dez to the West and the village of Serpil to the east. As for the Sat Mountains, entry to them happens through the Yeşiltaş "İştazın" or İkiyaka "Sat" villages.

The most suitable time for summer excursions and ascents to the Cilo-Sat Mountains are the months of June, July and August. The most suitable time for winter ascents are the months of February and March.

In this high mountainous area in the south-eastern tip of Turkey both rocky ground and glacier environments occupy broad areas.

Mountaineers will have to carry with them all the appropriate equipment, in accordance with their particular rock and glacier climbing programme.

Since the Cilo Mountains consist of massive limestone, they are suitable for climbings with pickets. The Sat Mountains, on the other hand, are not appropriate for this because of the cracked nature of their rocks. The effect of sun rays on the Cilo and Sat Mountains is very strong, and so excursion and climbing clothing should be chosen accordingly. Unguided excursions and climbing is not recommended on these mountains, since they occupy a very vast area.

On the Cilo-Sat Mountains there are no lodging facilities like mountain refuges or cottages. Every team of mountaineers should be sure to bring with it a sufficient number of sleeping bags and mountain tents. The high altitude "valley bottoms" in particular offer amenable climate conditions as well as plenty of drinking water. All the streams feeding from frozen snow and glaciers are constantly running and provide abundant clean water.

Before or after the excursions or ascents, those wishing to do so can stay in one of the two- or three-star hotels located in Hakkari and Yüksekova.

The Cilo-Sat Mountains are also the ideal place to observe semi-nomadic lifestyles. The highland life and regional clothing of the local people, who in summer move to high altitude pastures, are extremely interesting. The Cilo-Sat High Altitude Mountainous Area has in its entirety the characteristics of a "national park". Weaving carpets and similar textiles is a noteworthy activity typical of the area. One should not forget to buy a carpet or flat woven kilim when in the area.

For Further Details:

Turkish Mountaineering Federation
General Directorate for Youth and Sports
4th Floor Ulus / ANKARA
Phone: 0(312) 311 91 20 - Fax: 0(312) 310 15 78
E-mail: tdf1966@hotmail.com
Website: www.tdf.org.tr

Provincial Culture and Tourism Directorate, HAKKARİ
Phone: 0(438) 211 65 09 - Fax: 0(438) 211 27 52

KAÇKAR MOUNTAINS (3932 m.)

The Northern Anatolia mountain chains rising all along the Black Sea shore of the Anatolian peninsula, begin in the West with the Istıranca Mountains (1010 m.). They continue in the Western Black Sea Area as the Köroğlu (2400 m.) and the Ilgaz (2587 m.) mountains. These mountain chains, which continue in the Central Black Sea Area as the Karagöl and Çakırgöl mountains (3100 m.), acquire the name of Kaçkar Mountains once in the province of Rize and rise as high as 4000 metres.

These mountains rising between the Eastern Black Sea shores and the Çoruh River to the south, extend along a SW-NE axis. The Tatos Mountains, the Hunut Mountains, the Kaçkar Mountains, the Davut Mountains, the Güngörmez Mountains and the Altıparmak Mountains comprise main highest points of the Kaçkar Mountains. These mountains extend over an area measuring 80-100 km. in length and 40-50 km. in width.

Counting from the west to the east, the Varşamba "Verçenik" Mountains (3710 m.), the Kaçkar Mountains (3932 m.) and the Altıparmak Mountains (3492 m.) are the highest parts of these mountains. The highest peak of these mountains known as the Rize-Kaçkar Mountains is the Kaçkar-"Kavrun" Mountain (3932 m.).

The first scientific studies and publications about the Rize-Kaçkar Mountains were completed in 1949 by Dr. S. Erinç, and in 1952 by Dr. İ. Yalçınlar. Following these first studies by geographers and geologists, the Rize-Kaçkar Mountains began to arouse great interest both domestically and internationally. It is not known with certainty when the first summer ascent to the Kaçkar-Kavrun Mountain was carried out (3932 m.). However, the first "winter ascent" was done by Turkish mountaineers. Nine mountaineers led by Sönmez Targan and all members of the "Turkish Mountaineering Federation" ascended for the first time the Kaçkar-"Kavrun" Mountain (3932 m.) on 9th January 1974.

Geological Structure and Topography:

The formation of the land known as the Anatolian peninsula, which rose after being squeezed between the Arab Block and the Russian Massif, and which is part of the Alpine-Himalayan mountain formation, happened in the direction of north to south.

During these mountain formation movements and as a result of crumpling and breaking, the Northern Anatolian "Pontid" mountain chain and the Kaçkar Mountains, which are their extension of the former in the Eastern Black Sea Area, appeared, and the Black Sea depression to the north and the Caucasus Mountains even further north were formed.

The "Northern Anatolia Mountain Chain", which was formed when series dating to the Paleozoic and Lower-Mesozoic eras crumpled and broke, was probably the scene of intense eruptions from the nucleus during the Upper-Cretaceous era, especially in the area between the Çoruh River and the Black Sea, and following a very long-lasting erosion, the Rize-Kaçkar Mountains were formed by deep layer stones like granite, granodiorite and cyanite that surfaced and external eruption rocks of basaltic origin present especially in mid- and high-altitudes.

Erupted rocks made of basaltic lava present especially at mid- and high-altitudes led in general to the formation of rough and pointed summits with altitudes of more than 2800-3000 metres. These series, which dominate the environment in the mountains of Varşamba, Verçenik, Kavrun and Altıparmak, are present further east as series of diorite and andesite mixed with rocks like limestone and flysh of the Upper Cretaceous era.

The Kaçkar Mountains are have been violently eroded by rivers as well as by glaciers, both in the Ice age (Diluvial) of the Quaternary Period, a process which continues today. An irregular topography has appeared as a result of the fluvial and glacial erosion on these mountains. The intense freezing and melting phenomena that happen at high altitudes further accelerate the erosion and movements shaping these mountains.

These external forces, which have had an effect throughout many geological eras, have led the topography of the Kaçkar mountainous area to be fragmented, rough, high and forbidding. The Kaçkar mountainous area, where even today fluvial and glacial erosion is particularly powerful, is one of Turkey's most interesting areas, both with respect to its geological structure and young topography, and from the point of view of the morphology of its glaciers.

These mountains, which begin to rise close to the shore of the Black Sea, reach an altitude of 4000 metres at a distance of 40-50 km. from the shore. In coastal areas there are eroded slopes and ridges, and in places "terraced" formations of both marine and terrestrial origin. At higher altitudes there are plains cut by deep valleys.

These flat and eroded areas, which are covered with forests and cut by deep valleys, are replaced at altitudes higher than

1500 metres by high peneplains and plateaus also cut by plains. Above altitudes of 2100 metres, at which the forest cover ends, the high plateaus and forbidding peaks of the Kaçkar Mountains begin. Similar morphologic characteristics are present also on the southern slopes of these mountains.

Those parts of the Kaçkar Mountains with altitudes of more than 1500 metres are in general broken by glacier valleys, both ancient and relatively new. In between these valleys, which in places are as deep as 1000-1500 metres, there are plateaus and peneplains that are as as high as 3000 metres and occupy vast areas.

The northern slopes of the Kaçkar Mountains are steeper, rougher and more deeply cut by valleys than the southern slopes. This situation is due to differences in the geological structure and varying degrees of fluvial and glacial erosion. Among the typical manifestations of glacial erosion in the higher parts of the Kaçkar Mountains are glacier valleys both ancient and new, cirques in the upper parts of these valleys, glacier lakes and "moraine barriers" both ancient and new.

The glacier valleys on these mountains extending along a SW-NE axis are in general vertical to the axis of extension of the Kaçkar Mountains. The main glacier valleys, which are generally set along a NE axis on the northern and a SE axis on the southern slopes, are connected along their sides and upper parts to "hanging glacier" valleys. It has been observed that the lower ends of these valleys, which were formed in the Ice Age (Pleistocene) and which have maintained their morphologic structure to the present day, descend to 1600 metres on the southern slopes, and to 1400 metres on the northern slopes (İ. Yalçınlar, 1952).

The most important part of the Kaçkar Mountains, from the points of view of the geological structure, topography and mountaineering, consists of the Kaçkar "Kavrun" Mountains (3932 m.).

The erupted rocks that comprise the Kaçkar Mountains have are in general cracked in structure. It is because of this that the "freezing-melting phenomena", which happen especially in the summer, have a greater impact on the southern slopes, with the result that these slopes acquire a more rounded topography.

The Glacial Morphology of the Kaçkar Mountains:

The Kaçkar "Kavrun" Mountains, which comprise the highest parts of the Northern Anatolian mountain ranges and the Rize-Kaçkar Mountainous Region, are also an area of intense present-day glacier erosion and sedimentation.

While those parts of the Kaçkar "Kavrun" Mountains made up of rocks like granite, granodiorite and cyanite give rise to a truncated, flat topography, the parts made up of basaltic series have a sharper, more forbidding look. Similarly, while the northern slopes of the mountains have a more sheer and broken aspect because of fluvial and glacial erosion, the southern slopes have a flatter topography.

Glaciers on the Kaçkar Mountains, which were subjected to widespread, intense glacier erosion during the Quaternary Period Ice Age (Pleistocene), are found at altitudes as low as 2000-2050 metres. However, ancient and new glacial manifestations are apparent mostly at altitudes of 3000-3600 metres. It is also possible to observe glacial forms of both the Pleistocene "ice age" and of our days, on both the northern and the southern slopes of the Kaçkar-Kavrun Mountains.

The main examples of the areas where ancient and new manifestations of glaciers are present together, are the Heveg Valley on the south slopes of the Kaçkar "Kavrun" Mountains and the Kavrun Valley on the northern slope. Of the five mountain glaciers found on the Kaçkar Mountains, one is on the Varşamba "Verçenik" Mountains while the other 4 are on the Kaçkar Kavrun Mountains.

The "Great Glacier", which measures some 2 km. in length and 200-300 metres in width, and has a thickness of 30-40 metres, is located on the NW slope of the Kaçkar "Kavrun" Peak (3932 m.), beginning from an altitude of 3600 metres and extending down to 3000 metres.

Streams and Lakes "Hydrology"

The Kaçkar Mountains, which are located in the Eastern Black Sea region, a region which receives more rainfall than any other in Turkey (2400 mm.), are noteworthy for the density of their web of streams, abundance of water and plenitude of lakes. On the other hand, as a result of its geological structure, it is not rich in underground water sources.

The particular characteristics of these mountains derive from their varied altitudes, rough and forbidding topography and extreme inclinations. In addition, the fact that the southern and northern slopes of the Kaçkar Mountainous Area, the earth of which is non-permeable, should be covered with forests up to an altitude of 2100 metres, and with pastures and meadows above the limit of the forests, keeps surface water from seeping underground and gives rise to a web of streams with a strong current and plentiful water. It is for these natural characteristics that the Kaçkar Mountainous Area, where there is rain all through the year, has Turkey's richest flora and forests and fastest flowing web of streams.

The northward-running basin waters of the Rize-Kaçkar Mountains flow into the Black Sea by means of the Fırtına River. The Fırtına Stream feeding off of the glaciers and frozen snows on the north side of the Verçenik Peak, the Kavrun Stream feeding off of the glaciers and frozen snows of the Kavrun Mountains, and the Kaçkar Stream emptying the waters of the Altıparmak Mountains, are the main tributaries of the Fırtına River. The first two of these tributaries merge at Çamlıhemşin, creating the "Fırtına River". As for the waters of the Kaçkar Mountain's southward-facing basin, they flow into the Çoruh River by means of the Barhal Çayı, fed especially by the Heveg Stream and the Altıparmak Stream.

The Eastern Black Sea Rize-Kaçkar Mountains are a noteworthy area of Turkey with respect also to the formation and plentitude of glacier lakes. Many glacier lakes of various dimensions are widespread all over both the southern and northern slopes of the Kaçkar Mountainous Area. These lakes, which in general are located within the 2500-3000 metre altitude belt, were mostly formed by ancient and recent glacier erosion phenomena. The many glacier lakes on the Kaçkar Mountains and the "Büyükgöl" to the north of Heveg-Dilberdüzü are all examples of these mountain and glacier lakes.[8]

Thermal water sources are found on the Ayder Plateau (1250 m.), located on the northern slopes of the Kaçkar Mountains, which are particularly rich in terms of mineral deposits. The Ayder thermal water can be obtained from natural sources or drilled wells; it contains sodium sulphate and has a radioactive "2100 picokuri / litre" composition with "fountain of youth" characteristics, a temperature of $46°$C, a water output of 16 litres per second and a bath capacity of 2260 people per day (on the assumption of 600 litre consumption per person per day).

Natural Vegetation and Wildlife "Flora and Fauna"

The Kaçkar Mountains, which are located in an area with a year-round temperate and rainy climate, begin to rise near the Black Sea shore in the north, and in the Çoruh Valley in the south.

---

8 Heveg is the old name of the village of YAYLALAR located to the south of the Kaçkar "Kavrun" Mountains, and within the borders of Artvin-Yusufeli.

There are various belts of different vegetation, especially on the north slope, due to the fact that the mountains begin to rise very close to the shore. Tea and citrus is grown in the coastal area. These areas within the 0-750 metre altitude belt are densely covered with plants and have "broadleaf" forests. The main trees of this belt are broadleaf treas such as Chestnut (Castanea sativa), Beech (Carpinus betulus) and Fagus (Fagus orientalis).

As for the 750-1500 metre altitude belt, it contains mixed forests with both needleleaf and broadleaf trees. In this belt, apart from the above-mentioned broadleaf trees, there are also fir trees (Abies nurdmaniana) and coniferous trees like Spruce (Picea orientalis). Beyond 1500 metres there are only coniferous trees. Beyond 2100 metres there are meadows and pastures and an Alpine vegetation.

In the deep, large valleys on the south of the Kaçkar Mountains, which receive less rain and are sunnier in comparison to the north, and which constitute microclimates, there are "orchards and vineyards". Also in the case of the southern slopes of the mountains, there are both broadleaf and coniferous tree forests up to 1500 metres, and only coniferous tree forests above 1500 metres. Beyond the tree limit, which reaches an altitude of 2300 metres, there is a rich and varied cover of flowers and Alpine plants.

In particular, the pink and white forest rose "Rhododendron pontica", present from 1200 metres up to 2300-2500 metres, and the "Yellow Forest Rose" known as "Kumar", are typical of the area. The highlands of the Kaçkar Mountains, which look like a sea of forests, plateaus and mountains, are embellished by all kinds of flowers upon the arrival of summer. Below two thousand metres, in addition to the widespread yellow and pink forest roses and the saffrons, there are also campanulae, and beyond two thousand metres there are white forest roses, blue mountain saffrons, orchids and wild mountain lilies. The upper parts of the cool, abundant and fast flowing streams of the Kaçkar Mountains are suitable living and breeding environments for salmons. It is for this reason that the "Salmo trutta" salmon has found a spacious habitat in the streams of the Kaçkar Mountains.

Beekeeping is particularly widespread in the Kaçkar Mountains' forest belt between 1000-2000 metres and in the pastures and meadows up to the upper limit of forests at 2500 metres.

To neutralise the humidty of the soil in the Kaçkar Mountainous Area (especially in the forest belt at an altitude of 1000-2000 metres), bee hives are placed on high "Beech" trees. It is for this reason that the mountaineers visiting the Kaçkar Mountainous

Area use the term "Honey Mountains" for the Kaçkar Mountains. Another population symbolising wildlife on the Kaçkar Mountains is that of the local mountain goat (Capra orientalis), which grazes in herds on the high peaks.

Climatic Conditions and Climbing Seasons

The climate in the Eastern Black Sea coastal area is temperate and rainy. Here, daily and monthly temperature variations are very slight, and the yearly average temperature is 14°C. Tea and citrus fruits are cultivated, and the climate is sub-tropical temperate with rainfall year-round (2400 mm.).

In the summertime, masses of humid air warm up and expand during the day, and are then channeled towards deep valleys and rise towards the mountains. As they rise, these humid masses of air cool and grow dense, which in turn leads to "Avarız (extraordinary) rains". When there is no rain, on the other hand, the result is "fog". However, the occurrence of such weather, which happens during the day, especially in the afternoon, changes at night, when air masses growing cold and heavy are channeled towards deep valleys and extend downwards.

These air movements, which are occur primarily in the "rain zone" between the sea-shore and the altitude of 3000 metres, are replaced at higher altitudes by relatively sunny, less rainy atmospheric conditions. This notwithstanding, the high parts of the Kaçkar Mountains get plenty of rain in summer and winter. Places above an altitude of 1500 metres, where snowfall is at its most intense, receive 3-4 metres of snow per year.

As for the southern slopes of the Kaçkar Mountains, they are less affected by the "Avarız" rains observed in the northern slopes. It is for this reason that while summer in the northern parts of the mountains in general is rainy or foggy, on the southern slopes it is sunny and less rainy. Mountaineers wishing to carry out excursions or ascents on the Kaçkar Mountains have to prepare a programme that takes into consideration these climatic conditions. Since there are no meteorological stations in the area of the Kaçkar Mountains, climatic data for Rize and Yusufeli have been indicated in the following table.

The most suitable time for summer ascents in this mountainous area is August and September, while for winter ascents it is the months of February and March. The months of June and July on the other hand are partially rainy and foggy (in the north).

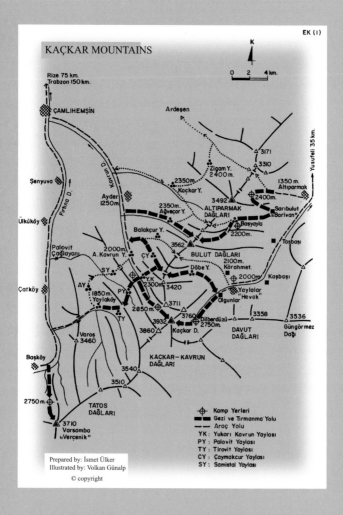

Name of the Station: Rize
Altitude: 0.4 m.

	I	II	III	IV	V	VI	VII	VIII	IX	X	XI	XII	Yıl
Average monthly temperature (C°)	7	7	8	11	16	20	22	23	20	16	13	9	14
Sunny and partially sunny days/month	16	14	16	16	19	21	21	18	18	20	18	18	212
Average number of snow-covered days/month	5	5	5	-	-	-	-	-	-	-	-	2	14
Greatest thickness of snow-cover (cm.)	187	95	52	21	-	-	-	-	-	-	29	50	187
Average monthly relative humidity	73	75	76	79	81	79	81	82	82	80	78	73	78

Source: Bulletin of the State General Directorate of Meteorological Affairs.

Name of the Station: Yusufeli
Altitude: 611 m.

	I	II	III	IV	V	VI	VII	VIII	IX	X	XI	XII	Yıl
Average monthly temperature (C°)	4	5	10	15	19	23	26	26	22	15	10	5	15
Sunny and partially sunny days/month	22	22	24	24	27	29	30	29	28	26	22	23	308
Average number of snow-covered days/month	2	3	-	-	-	-	-	-	-	-	1	2	8
Greatest thickness of snow-cover (cm.)	12	30	6	-	-	-	-	-	-	-	35	20	35
Average monthly relative humidity	68	62	58	72	60	66	60	58	55	60	64	70	63

Source: Bulletin of the State General Directorate of Meteorological Affairs.

EXCURSIONS AND CLIMBING IN THE KAÇKAR MOUNTAINS

The Rize-Kaçkar Mountainous Area extending along a SW-NE axis, rises in three parts. In the Eastern part of the Kaçkar Mountains there are the Altıparmak Mountains. The highest peaks of these mountains are the Karataş (3492 m.) and Altıparmak (3307 m.) peaks.

To the west of the Altıparmak Mountains there are the Bulut and Kaçkar "Kavrun" mountains. The highest peak of the Bulut Mountains is Kuşaklıkaya (3562 m.), while the highest peak of the Kaçkar Mountains is the Kaçkar "Kavrun" Peak (3932 m.). To the east of the Kavrun Mountains rise the Mezovit Mountains.

To the west of the Kavrun Mountains are the Tatos Mountains. The highest peak of these mountains is the Varşamba "Verçenik" (3710 m.) peak. The highest peaks of the Kaçkar Mountains and the routes of ascent to these peaks have been indicated on the maps.

Climbing the Altıparmak and Kavrun Mountains from the South Side

For an ascent to the Altıparmak and Kaçkar "Kavrun" Mountains from the south side, the Altıparmak Mountains have to be entered through the Erzurum-Yusufeli-Sarıgöl-Altıparmak village of "Barhal". The Erzurum-Yusufeli highway passes along the western side of Tortum Lake, which is an "avalanche barrier lake". The Tortum Lake's geological and morphological structure is definitely worth seeing. The distance between Erzurum and Yusufeli is 135 km. After spending the night at Yusufeli, visitors will go to the Altıparmak "Barhal" Village for an ascent up the Altıparmak Mountains, and to the Yaylalar "Heveg" Village for an ascent up the Kaçkar "Kavrun" Mountain (3932 m.). Yusufeli and the Altıparmak Village are 33 km. apart while the distance between Yusufeli and the Altıparmak-Yaylalar Village is 65 km.[9]

In Yusufeli there is a "guesthouse" for mountaineers and hunters. It is possible to secure lodging there for a small fee. In addition, there are new, good quality lodging facilities in the county seats, and also lodging houses in the Altıparmak "Barhal" and Yaylalar "Hevag" villages.

The ascent up the Altıparmak Mountains begins by going to the Barhal Village on foot. Equipment is carried on pack animals. Following a four hour trip, camp is set up on the Naznara Plateau to the south of the Altıparmak Mountains, or near the lake of Karagöl (2500 m.). The peaks of Altıparmak rise above the western and northwestern side of the camp site. The mountaineers, after resting and carrying out excursions here for a day, will determine their route of ascent according to their own ability and experience.

---

9 The Kaçkar Mountains' southern slopes are within the borders of Yusufeli County in Artvin Province, in an area which used to be known as "Livane".

Mountaineers who have completed their excursions and ascents up the Altıparmak Mountains, will either cross the "Büyükkapı Pass" and go to the northern side of the Altıparmak

Mountains or climb to Başyayla via Sarıbulut "Borivan". Having spent the night at one of these destinations, on the the following day mountaineers will proceed to the Kaçkar Plateau via the "Hızarkapı Pass" and to the Ağveçor "Avusor" Plateau via the Kırmızıgedik Pass. Both plateaus are on the northern side of the Altıparmak Mountains and within the borders of Çamlıhemşin County, and both plateaus have an altitude of around 2300 metres.

Local guides are absolutely necessary during the passage from the southern slopes of the Kaçkar Mountains, which in general are clear and sunny, to the northern slopes, which at times are foggy and rainy. Otherwise, there is always the possibility of losing your way and getting turned around or caught up in "blind alleys". Mountaineers who have reached the Ayder Thermal Sources via the "Hızarkapı" or "Kırmızıgedik" passes and then the Avusor Plateau, will from there go to the Kaçkar "Kavrun" Mountains. The Başyayla-Avusor Plateau-Ayder Thermal Sources route lasts around 7-8 hours. During these passages a "Trans Kaçkar" route will have been followed.

Ascent Up the Kaçkar-Kavrun Mountain (3932 m.) Along the South Slope

Mountaineers wishing to climb the Kaçkar "Kavrun" Mountain (3932 m.) from the south side, will go by car through the village of Altıparmak to the village of Yaylalar "Heveg". The distance between Altıparmak and the village of Yaylalar is 33 km. The road is narrow and of compressed earth. In the village of Yaylalar there is a village clinic, new lodging houses and a "mountain refuge".

The trek for the ascent up the Kaçkar-Kavrun Mountain will begin at the Yaylalar (Heveg) Village. After having crossed the Olgunlar "Meretet" area and climbed the valley, camp will be set up at an altitude of 2750 metres, in a place known as Dilberdüzü. It takes around 3-4 hours to travel from the village of Yaylalar to Dilberdüzü on foot. The load and equipment will be carried on pack animals, which can be found at the village of Yaylalar.

The Kaçkar "Kavrun" Mountain (3932 m.) is to the north-east of the campsite. Mountaineers who leave the campsite in the morning can return on the same day, after having seen the Deniz Lake "Great Lake" or having directly climbed the peak.

To the northwest of the Dilberdüzü campsite is the Sönmeztepe (3860 m.) peak. This peak is accessible from the glacier on its eastern side or from the ridge on its southern side.

Following the ascent to the peak, mountaineers will pass through the Olgunlar area, the Döbe Plateau and the "Lanetleme Geçidi" (Damnation Pass) to the Upper Çaymakçur Plateau, and through the Körahmat Plateau to the Balakçur Plateau, all of which generally takes 6-8 hours. As in the case of the Altıparmak Mountains, use of a "local guide" is an absolute necessity. It is also recommended that excursions and ascents be suspended during foggy and rainy weather and that teams wait such weather out at the campsite.

Mountaineers who arrive at the Çaymakçur or Palakçur plateaus will reach the Kaçkar "Kavrun" Mountains via the Kavrun Plateau.

Ascents Up the Kaçkar Mountains From the North

The Trabzon-Rize Çamlıhemşin highway, a 150 km-long, asphalt-paved highway, is used to reach the point suitable for ascent up the Kaçkar Mountains from the north. The most suitable approach and entrance point from the North for the Kaçkar Mountains is the Çamlıhemşin-Ayder Thermal Source. The distance between Çamlıhemşin and Ayder is 16 km. The road is paved with asphalt.

Final preparations for excursions and ascents up the Kaçkar-Altıparmak or Kaçkar-Kavrun mountains are done at the Ayder Thermal Source. Ayder, with an altitude of around 1250 m., is a beautiful plateau and thermal resort where one can find a number of quality lodging facilities and places to eat.

Climbing the Altıparmak Mountains from the North

To climb the Altıparmak Mountains from the north, mountaineers have first to go from the Ayder Thermal Source to the Ağveçor or "Avusor" Plateau. This trek will last 3-4 hours. It is possible to climb to the plateau using all-terrain vehicles and minibuses.

Camp is set up near the 2300 metre-high Avusor Plateau. From there it is possible to climb to the "Kemerlikaçkar" peaks (3562 m.).

For ascents from the north to the other high peaks on the Altıparmak Mountains, mountaineers will go through the Kaçkar Plateau further east to the Ambar Lake (2750 m.), where camp will be set up. From that campsite mountaineers might go east to climb also the Kaçkar-Altıparmak Mountains' Karataş Peak (3492 m.).

Traversing the distance between the Avusor Plateau and the Ambar Lake will take 3-4 hours on foot. Once they have set up camp on Ambar Lake, mountaineers will determine the peaks they want to climb and their routes of ascent, according to weather conditions and their own abilities and experience.

Mountaineers who have finished their excursions and ascents up the Altıparmak Mountains can do a "Trans-Kaçkar" through the Upper Kaçkar Plateau-Hızarkapı or the Avusor Plateau Kırmızı-Gedik passes, and pass on to the south side of the Kaçkar Mountains, from whence they can descend to the village of Barhar and to Yusufeli, or they can return to the Kaçkar "Kavrun" Mountains via the Ağveçor "Avusor" Plateau and Ayder.

Climbing the Kaçkar-Kavrun Mountain (3932 m.) from the North Slope

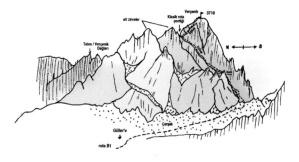

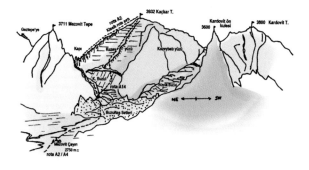

The Kaçkar "Kavrun" Mountain (3932 m.) is the highest peak of these mountains. To climb the Kaçkar-Kavrun Mountain, mountaineers will have to follow the Ayder Thermal Source-

Lower Kavrun Plateau and go to the Upper Kavrun Plateau either on foot or by motor vehicle. (This rough road is 12 km. long.) From the Upper Kavrun Plateau a two-hour trek will take mountaineers to the place known as Boğaçayırı or Öküzçayırı located at an altitude of 2800 metres, where camp will be set up. Right beside the camp to the east are the "Mezovit points", while to its south rises the "Büyük Kaçkar", or the "Kavrun Peak" (3932 m.). Mountaineers will rest here for a day and carry out excursions to nearby surroundings. These can also serve as reconaissance tours for the ascent to the peak.

There are 3 routes that can be followed to climb the Kaçkar "Kavrun" Mountain along its northern slope. Mountaineers can climb to the peak either along the Great Glacier or along the central ridge of the northern slope of the Kaçkar "Kavrun" Mountain or by climbing towards the west along the ridges east of the Lesser Glacier. Mountaineers wishing to ascend to the peak along the Great Glacier, should have with them ice axes, ice irons, mountain ropes, rope ladders and ice pegs. Ascent up the Kaçkar-Kavrun Mountain (3932 m.) from the campsite at Öküzçayırı "Boğaçayırı" and return will under normal conditions last 8-10 hours.

Mountaineers who have completed their Kaçkar-Kavrun ascent, might, if they so wish, carry out ascents to the peaks called Mezovit (rising to the east of the Boğaçayırı campsite), which have degrees of difficulty varying between four and six.

Excursions and Ascents up Mount Verçenik

To reach the Varşamba "Verçenik" Peak (3710 m.) at the extreme west of the Kaçkar Mountains, mountaineers will first have to go to Ortaköy through Çamlıhemşin and Çat. This road, which is a service road of the forest management service, is around 25 km. long. Ortaköy is a plateau and village to the north of Mount Verçenik. It is reached from Çamlıhemşin by means of minibuses or 4x4s. Camp is set up on the İşmer Plateau on the northern slopes of Mount Verçenik. This trek lasts around one hour. Each mountaineer will determine his or her own route of ascent to the Verçenik "Varşamba" Peak (3710 m.). Ascent to the peak lasts around six hours. Return to the camp takes place on the same day.

People who begin their excursions and ascents up the Kaçkar Mountains at the Mount Verçenik, will travel by 4x4s from the village of Çat to the Elevit Plateau, and from there to the Tirovit Plateau. The trip from the Tirovit Plateau to the Palovit Tableau

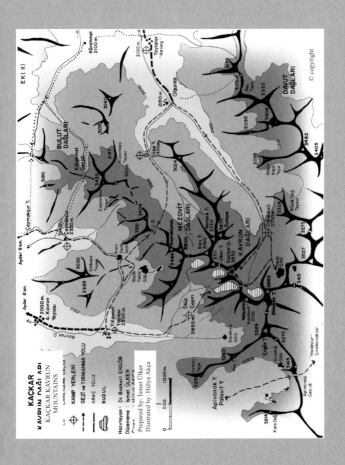

can be done either on foot or by motor vehicle, but the trip from the Palovit Tableau to the Upper Kavrun Plateau can be done only on foot. However, these passages should not be done without a guide.

Excursion and Ascent Programme for the Kaçkar Mountains

First Alternative "Trans Kaçkar"

1st day: Erzurum-Yusufeli.

2nd day: Yusufeli-Altıparmak Village

61

3rd day: Altıparmak campsite (2500 m.)

4th day: Altıparmak "Karataş" ascent (3492 m.)

5th day: Altıparmak-Başyayla

6th day: Başyayla-Kaçkar or Avusor Plateau

Second Alternative "Trans Kaçkar"

1st day: Erzurum-Yusufeli.

2nd day: Yusufeli-Yaylalar "Heveg" Village.

3rd day: Heveg Village-Dilberdüzü (2750 m.)

4th day: Dilberdüzü campsite.

5th day: Büyükgöl-Kaçkar (3932 m.) Peak.

6th day: Dilberdüzü-Döbe Plateau.

7th day: Döbe Plateau, Çaymakçur Plateau, Ayder.

Third Alternative

1st day: Trabzon-Rize-Çamlıhemşin-Ayder.

2nd day: Ayder-U. Kavrun Plateau-Öküzçayırı campsite.

3rd day: Excursions and rest at the camp site (2800 m.).

4th day: Kaçkar "Kavrun" ascent (3932 m.).

5th day: Return trip or Ayder-Çamlıhemşin-Verçenik.

Updated Information and Recommendations

The Erzurum-Yusufeli-Altıparmak highway (170 km.) will be used to approach the Kaçkar Mountains from the south. As for the approach to the mountains from the north, this is done via the Trabzon-Rize-Çamlıhemşin-Ayder route, which is 166 km. long. The roads along this route are paved in asphalt until Yusufeli and Ayder, and thereafter are comprised of compressed earth.

The best time for ascents up the Kaçkar Mountains are the months of August and September. In the months of June and July the northern slopes can be a bit rainy or foggy, while the southern slopes get less rain, and are in general clear and sunny. Teams planning to carry out excursions and ascents along the northern slopes of the Kaçkar Mountains should be certain to bring along their raincoats.

Since rocks are cracked and there is active freezing and melting happening, ascents to these peaks are not suitable for the use of pegs and ropes. In addition to this, mountaineers or trekkers must beware of loose and rolling stones even during normal ascents. As for those planning to carry out excursions or ascents on the glaciers, they should have with them ice pickaxes, ice

pegs, rope ladders and mountain ropes. Peak ascents should be avoided in foggy weather.

There are "mountain refuges" in the villages of Altıparmak and Yaylalar on the southern slopes of the Kaçkar Mountains, as well as on the Upper Kavrun Plateau on the northern slopes, and good quality lodging facilities in Yusufeli and on the Ayder Plateau too. However, there are no mountain refuges at the campsites. Sleeping bags and mountain tents are therefore necessary for spending the night.

The northern and southern parts of the Kaçkar Mountains in particular constitute a "national park" of worldwide importance, thanks to its particular structural characteristics, rich flora and forests. Seasonal migrations to the highlands in the mountainous areas within the borders of the "Kaçkar Mountains National Park", and in particular festivities celebrating the "ascent" and "return" from the highland plateaus are worth seeing. The horon folk dance to the accompaniment of bagpipes known as "tulum zurna" are also very interesting and typical of the area. The Eastern Black Sea Area is famous for its "highland and horon" festivities.

For Further Details:

Turkish Mountaineering Federation
General Directorate for Youth and Sports
4th Floor , Ulus / ANKARA
E-mail: tdf1966@hotmail.com
Website: www.tdf.org.tr
Phone: 0(312) 311 91 20 - Fax: 0(312) 310 15 78

Culture and Tourism Directorate
Building of the Governor's Office 5th Floor, RİZE
Phone: 0(464) 213 04 07 - Fax: 0(464) 213 04 06
E-mail: rizekulturturizm@ttnet.tr

TAURUS-ALADAĞLAR (3771 m.)

The Taurus Mountains located on the Alpine-Himalayan mountain belt, are of the four main tectonic units comprising Turkey. These folded mountain chains, referred to by geographers as the "Taurids", surround the Anatolian peninsula from the south.

The Taurus Mountains, which have a very rough, high and forbidding topography, are made up of four main parts: the Western Tauruses, the Central Tauruses, the Eastern Tauruses and the South-eastern Tauruses. The highest peaks of the Taurus Mountains are located in the Central Tauruses and in the South-eastern Tauruses.

The Central Tauruses are made up of two parts. The part of these mountains that lies between the Göksu River and the Pozantı Stream is known as the Bolkar Mountains (3524 m.), while the part between the Çamardı-Ecemiş Stream and the Zamantı River is known as the Aladağlar (3771 m.).

The Aladağlar, which are the highest part of the Central Tauruses, are located within the provinces of Kayseri, Niğde and Adana. The greater part of these mountains lies within Çamardı County in the province of Niğde; to their west flows the Ecemiş Stream, and to their east the Zamantı River. On the Ecemiş Stream which delineates the western border of the Aladağlar, are the villages of Çukurbağ and Demirkazık.

The Aladağlar, which extend along a SW-NE axis, cover an area measuring around 50 km. in length and 25-30 km. in width. The highest peaks of these mountains are the Demirkazık Peak (3758 m.) in the north, Kızılkaya (3771 m.) in the centre, the Kaldı Peak (3688 m.) in the south, and Vayvay Tepe (3565 m.) in the east. The south-eastern part of the Aladağlar, which is located within Adana province, is known as the Turasan or "Turhasan" Mountains.

Geological Structure and Topography

The Taurus-Aladağlar on the Alpine-Himalayan folded mountain belt are made up primarily of rocks of the Mesozoic (Upper cretaceous) era. These sedimentary layers with a thickness of 1500-2000 metres, consist of limestone, dolomitic (chalk stone) and ophiolitic series.

The Aladağlar, which are a folded mountain chain, have an average altitude of 3500 metres, and an overlayered "napped" structure. The layers of the Aladağlar, which rise in between the valleys of Ecemiş and Barazama, generally run or are inclined in a south-easterly direction. The "nappes", having formed in connection with the inclining and curving movements of the layers, therefore run in the same direction. The main tectonic units making up the main geological structure of the Aladağlar are explained in brief below.

The Black Aladağlar

The "Black Aladağ" series to the north of the Aladağlar are of the Paleozoic era. These series have quartzite intermediate layers, and are made up of chalk stone (limestone and dolomitic) with clay stone and shale alternation.

The Ecemiş Depression

The Ecemiş depression situated along a NS axis is located between the Aladağlar and the Niğde Massif. The Ecemiş depression was formed as a result of a forward moving fault line. This depression, which has affected the geological strata of the Quaternary Period, is a "fault line" still active today. The river terracces on the valley slopes of the Ecemiş Stream are the product of these active tectonic movements.

The Çukurbağ Layers

In between the Ecemiş depression and the Aladağlar are the "Çukurbağ layers". These series, which measure 5-10 km. in width and are located between the village of Çukurbağ and the western slopes of the Aladağlar, consist of an alternation of clay stone, sandstone and conglomerate. Located between the Ecemiş fault line and the Aladağlar, the series is in places as thick as 600 metres.

The White Aladağ Layers

These series comprising the Aladağlar high mountainous area consist of white-grey limestone and dolomites ($CaMgSO$). The White Aladağ layers of the Trias-Jura era are concentrated between the Çukurbağ Layers and the Barazama Valley. The highest peaks of the Central Tauruses rise above this "napped series", the thickness of which is more than 1500 metres.

The Aladağ Ophiolitic Series

These series are made up of serpentine rocks with fliche and conglomerate at their base, and of chalk stones with intermediate layers of pyroxene, gabro and radiolarite. Magmatic and metamorphic in origin, they can be observed in all "nappes". The layered nappes of the White Aladağ Layer and of the Aladağ

Ophiolitic Series, which comprise the main structure of the Taurus-Aladağlar, can be observed at the point where the Hacer Valley and the Kapuzbaşı Village underground streams reach the surface.

Morphologic Characteristics of the Aladağlar

There are four main elevations on the Aladağlar, which are high and folded mountain chains. These elevations are respectively the Demirkazık, Yedigöller, Kaldı and Turasan mountains. To the extreme north of the Aladağlar lies Demirkazık. The Demirkazık (3758 m.) Mountain is the second highest peak of the Aladağlar. At the centre of the Aladağlar lies the Yedigöller Valley. The Kızılkaya (3771 m.) Mountain is the highest peak of this area and of the Aladağlar. To the South are the Kaldı Mountain elevations. As for this area, its highest peak is the Kaldı Mountain (3688 m.). The south-eastern part of the Aladağlar consists of the Turasan Mountains. The highest mountain of this area is Vayvay Tepe (3665 m.).

Glacier Morphology

The summits of the Aladağlar are above the "year-round snow" limit, which is located at an altitude of around 3000 metres. It is for this reason that on the Aladağlar, contemporary glacier topography and glacier remains from the Diluvial "Pleistocene" era can coexist. On the Aladağlar, intense freezing-melting movements continue along with frozen snow and glacier erosion. Both the ancient and new glacier topography of the Aladağlar can be seen in the Çımbar Valley, the Yedigöller Valley (3100 m.), the Hacer and Mangırcı valleys and the Sıyırma Pass, all of which are actually ancient glacier valleys. In and over these valleys, which possess typical "vessel valley" glacier valley characteristics, you can see both ancient and new "cirque" bowls, glacier sediments, moraines and glacier lakes.

It is possible to see even nowadays many cirque bowls and a few glacier nuclei embedded in them in the upper parts of these ancient valleys. Two of them are in the Yedigöller Valley, at an altitude of around 3200-3400 metres, embedded between the Karagöl Ridge and Kızılkaya.

Karst Morphology

The geological layers of the Aladağlar are made up of erodable stones like limestone and dolomite. The porous and erodable stones (especially under the effect of rain and surface water) make for an environment that is extremely suitable for the formation and shaping of a Karst morphology. And indeed, on the Aladağlar there are not only many surface manifestations of the Karst topography, but also interesting and majestic elements of underground Karst topography (like underground lakes and streams).

The fact that underground Karst streams collecting the surface water of a great part of the Aladağlar and in particular of the Yedigöller Valley should surface on the eastern side of the mountain near the village of Kapuzbaşı forming waterfalls is an interesting example of "Underground Karst" and of the connected Karst hydrography. Another example of such surfacing of underground Karst streams can be found in the village of Demirkazık.

Notwithstanding the height and roughness of the Aladağlar, their geological structure has diminished the effectiveness of fluvial erosion and sedimentation. It is freezing-melting phenomena that are more effective on the Aladağlar as a result of the existence of a Karst and glacier topography. As a consequence of this, there are piles of sedimentation pebbles, "çarşak", which have flown down the slopes and accumulated over vast areas, especially on the slopes.

Physical phenomena like the erosion of glaciers and frozen snow as well as freezing-melting have been in effect on the Aladağlar ever since the ice age. The north-facing slopes of the mountains have acquired a rough and high look, while the south-facing slopes, where only freezing-melting and surface sweeping are in effect, have acquired a less steep look, with regular and not particularly rough surfaces.

Streams and Lakes: "Hydrology"

Fluvial erosion in the northern, central and southern parts of the Aladağlar is not very effective, and hence does not mark the topography of these areas. As a result of the geological structure and topography, streams are not very big or widespread. As for the Ecemiş Suyu to the west of the Aladağlar and the fast flowing stream to the east of the mountain, they are the result of the surfacing of Karst streams deriving from the nature of the above- and underground Karst topography.

Examples of surfacing water sources are those found in the villages of Demirkazık and Ecemiş and which are the primary sources feeding the Ecemiş Stream, as well as the Kapuzbaşı underground stream, which also surfaces in several locations.

At the bottoms of the valleys of Çımbar, Yedigöller and Karagöl, where glacial and Karst topography is particularly dominant, we find lakes. These lakes formed by the erosion of frozen snow, glaciers and also karstic phenomena, are also "water swallowing" bowls. These lakes formed due to melting and external forces can also be described as "glacio-karst" formations, just like the Dipsiz Lake in Çımbar Valley, Büyükgöl in the Yedigöller Valley and Karagöl in the Turasanlar Area.

The Aladağlar are not very rich as far as underground water sources are concerned. The few places where underground water sources surface are generally those used as highland settlements and campsites and refuges for mountaineers. Examples include "Sokulupınar" on the western slope of Demirkazık Mountain, or "Akşampınarı" and "Sulağankeler" on the slopes of Kaldı Mountain.

Natural Vegetation and Wildlife "Flora and Fauna"

The Aladağlar, which are located in the area of transition between the hot Mediterranean climate and the Central Anatolia continental climate, are not very rich in terms of forests. Due to their altitude, part of the Aladağlar lies above the forest limit. Forests are present only in Emli Valley and in the lower parts of Hacer Pass. The forests in the Hacer Pass consist of Yellow Pine "Pinus silvester" and Cedar "Cedres libanis", while those in the Emli Valley are made up of Black Pine "Pinus nigra" and Fir "Abies sp.".

The Aladağlar, the higher parts of which are within the Alpine vegetation belt, are a particularly rich and fascinating area as far as plant species are concerned. Among the mountain flowers typical to this area are the Taurus carnation and the snowdrop as well as the tragacanth, which is typical of the Hacer Pass.

Primary amongst wild and game animals living in the area are "mountain goats". The mountain goat "Capra hircus", which became an endangered species as a result of excessive hunting, was placed under the protection of the "National Parks Agency" of the Ministry of the Environment and Forests. Apart from the goats, other wild animals present in the area are wildcats, wolves, boars, foxes and rabbits. As for the avian presence, the Golden Eagle, the Booted Eagle and the Caspian Snowcock (Tetraogallus caspius) are important species inhabiting the area.

Climate and Climbing Seasons

The Aladağlar, which are located between the Mediterranean Basin, where summers are dry and hot, and winters temperate and rainy, and the Central Anatolian Basin, where summers are dry and hot, and winters partially rainy, carry traces of the climatic conditions of both basins.

Because of very high altitude (3500 m. on average), winter precipitations on the Aladağlar consist of snowfall, while in the summer there is a dry climate and sun raysa re particularly powerful. This situation proves that the Aladağlar are more under the influence of the Mediterranean climate rather than the Central Anatolian climate. Notwithstanding these climatic conditions, the months of June, July and August are the most suitable times for excursions and ascents. The months of April and May are not recommended because of the danger of avalanches, and the months of September and October because of a lack of water on the mountains and hence little in the way of flourishing nature. (The data of the Niğde Meteorology station, which is the nearest to the Aladağlar, have been indicated below.)

Mountaineers and nature lovers who plan to climb or ski on the Aladağlar in early summer should be wary of "sliding avalanches", especially in April and May, and in early winter, that is, in November and December, of "breaking avalanches", which are extremely dangerous. Those wishing to go to the Aladağlar for mountaineering or ski excursions are advised to visit during the period between 20th January and 20th March as the snow cover is most stable at that time.

Name of Station: Niğde
Altitude: 1208 m.

	I	II	III	IV	V	VI	VII	VIII	IX	X	XI	XII	Yıl
Average monthly temperature (C°)	0	1	5	10	15	19	22	22	18	12	7	2	11
Sunny and partially sunny days/month	21	20	23	25	28	29	31	31	29	28	26	21	312
Average number of snow-covered days/month	12	8	3	-	-	-	-	-	-	-	1	6	29
Greatest thickness of snow-cover (cm.)	34	25	30	4	-	-	-	-	-	-	30	26	34
Average monthly relative humidity	70	68	62	55	53	46	40	38	44	55	64	70	55

Source: Bulletin of the State General Directorate of Meteorological Affairs.

EXCURSIONS AND ASCENTS UP THE ALADAĞLAR

Mountaineers wishing to carry out excursions and ascents up the Aladağlar, will in general approach the mountains via the Niğde-Çamardı-Çukurbağ Village Route. Those wishing to climb to the Demirkazık Peak or to trek in the Çımbar Valley only will enter through the village of Demirkazık.

The Niğde-Çamardı highway (65 km.) is used to reach the village of Çukurbağ. This highway is paved with asphalt. Travellers using the Niğde-Çamardı buses will get off at the village of Çukurbağ, which is on the highway, six km. before Çamardı. After having completed preparations at Çukurbağ, mountaineers will then make their way to the Aladağlar.

However, mountaineers wishing to climb Demirkazık only, or certain groups of mountaineers wishing to rest, will go to the village of Demirkazık. The distance between the villages of Çukurbağ and Demirkazık is around five km. The road is compressed earth. In the village of Demirkazık there are "mountain refuges" with a total capacity of 81 beds and a "sports training centre" with 60 beds, all of which are open year-round.

Researchers and mountaineers wishing to carry out excursions or ascents up these mountains for the first time, will have to take steps to protect themselves against strong sunlight in all of the mountainous area. Light coloured cotton clothes should be used during excursions and ascents.

Excursions and ascents up the Aladağlar will in general be carried out in four parts. These excursions and ascents will be programmed as the Demirkazık, Yedigöller, Kaldı and Turasan ascents, in that order. Mountaineers wishing to carry out excursions and ascents up the Aladağlar, where forbidding and high peaks are near to each other, should be very careful, even during the simplest looking excursion. Transport, first aid and evacuation activities in this high mountainous area which extends over a vast space are carried out either with great difficulty or not at all. It is for this reason that one should be absolutely sure to avoid risky behaviour.

Excursion and trek routes on the Aladağlar and also campsites and ascent routes have been indicated on the map.

Ascent to Demirkazık (3758 m.)

The first summer ascent to the Demirkazık Peak was carried out on 17th July 1927 by Dr. G. Künne and his team. As for the first winter ascent, it was completed on 29th February 1969 by Dr. Bozkurt Ergör and Sönmez Targan.

The Sokulupınar campsite is generally used for ascents to Demirkazık, which is the second highest peak of the Aladağlar. There is always water at the campsite. The Sokulupınar campsite is located at a distance of around two hours on foot from the Çukurbağ and Demirkazık villages. This campsite will be used for normal ascents to the Demirkazık Peak from the south-east and south slopes and for the "ascent up the western slope", which poses technical difficulties.

The Narpuz Valley will be used for normal ascents to Demirkazık along the south-eastern and southern slopes. Once the more or less centre of this valley is reached, either a northward turn will be made and the ascent to the peak will be carried out along the southern slope or the trek will continue until the end of the Narpuz Valley. At the end of the valley, the "Kızılçarşak" slope, which covered in piles of pebbles, is climbed and the first ridge is reached. The south-east side of the ridge leading to the peak is followed until the peak is reached.

Once the peak has been reached, the team will return to the campsite following the route of ascent. Under normal conditions, ascents to the peak will last 8-10 hours.

Some teams set up an intermediate camp after entrance to the Narpuz Valley and after having passed a narrow pass at an altitude of 2500 metres. At this location, which is known as Kayacık and situated on the right-hand slope of the valley, there is a constant spply of water.

Ascent to the Demirkazık Peak (3758 m.)
Along the Western and Southern Slopes

Ascents to the Demirkazık Peak along the western and northern slopes require ability and experience. In particular, mountaineers, who are not good at "ascent by rope and pegs" should not attempt to climb from these sides.

The "Sokulupınar" campsite will be used for ascent along the western slope to the Demirkazık Mountain (3758 m.). Each mountaineer will determine the route of ascent according to his or her own ability and experience.

For an ascent to Demirkazık along the northern slope, the team will go to the Çımbar Valley via the Arpalık Plateau. An intermediate camp will be set up there. The distance between Sokulupınar and the Çımbar Valley will be covered on foot in 4-5 hours. Mountaineers, who have set up camp at the Çımbar Valley will determine their own routes of ascent. In general, ascent to Demirkazık along the northern slope is more difficult than ascent along the western slope. The grade of difficulty of ascents is in general 4-6. Mountaineers who have climbed from this side will follow the south-eastern ridge and descend back to the Çımbar Valley.

Ascents to the Peak Along the Yedigöller Valley

To reach the Yedigöller Valley (3100 m.), the trek will begin at the village of Çukurbağ or at the campsite of Sokulupınar. In

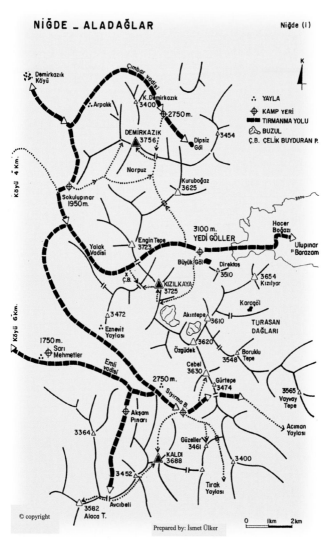

NİĞDE – ALADAĞLAR

Niğde (I)

K

∴ YAYLA
⊕ KAMP YERI
▰▰ TIRMANMA YOLU
🏔 BUZUL
Ç.B. CELİK BUYDURAN P.

Demirkazık Köyü

Çımbar vadisi

Arpalık

K.Demirkazık 3400

2750 m.

DEMİRKAZIK ▲ 3756

Dipsiz Göl

△3454

Narpuz

Kuruboğaz 3625

Köyü 4 Km.

Sokulupınar 1950 m.

3100 m. YEDİ GÖLLER

Hacer Boğazı

Engin Tepe 3723

Yalak Vadisi

Ulupınar "Barazam

Büyük Göl

Direktaş 3510

Ç.B.

▲ KIZILKAYA 3725

△3654 Kızılyar

Karagöl

△3472

Akıntepe △3610

TURASAN DAĞLARI

Köyü 6 Km.

Eznevit Yaylası

Özgüdek

△3620

Boruklu Tepe 3548

1750 m.
Sarı Mehmetler

Emli vadisi

Cebel 3630

Gürtepe △ 3474

3565 △ Vayvay Tepe

2750 m.

Sıyırma B.

Akşam Pınarı

Acıman Yaylası

3364△

Güzeller 3461△

KALDI ▲ 3688

△3400

△3452

Tırak Yaylası

© copyright

△3582 Alaca T.

Avcıbeli

Prepared by: İsmet Ülker

0   1km   2km

around two hours, the entrance to the Yalak Valley will be reached. The trek will continue along the Yalak Valley, all the while climbing towards the east. At the end of the valley, a northward turn will be made and trekking will continue until the Çelikbuyduran Source is reached. The team will rest there.

Following the rest, the ridge will be passed and the entrance to the Yedigöller Valley will be reached. A descent lasting around one hour will bring the team to the lakes area at an altitude of 3100 metres. Camp will be set up along the shores or near the Great Lake (Büyük Göl). The distance between Çukurbağ and the Yedigöller campsite will be traversed by trekking which will last around 6-8 hours.

The Yedigöller has its own micro climate. Due to the altitude, the water will freeze during the night at the Yedigöller Valley campsite. As for daytime, sun rays will be extremely intense and burning. Because of a difference between nighttime and daytime temperatures of 25-30°C, mountaineers will have to be especially careful to safeguard themselves against strong rays.

Ascent from the Yedigöller Valley to Kızılkaya (3771 m.)

The Kızılkaya Peak rises to the south-west of the Yedigöller Valley. Kızılkaya, the northern part of which is very rough and high, is the highest peak of the Aladağlar. Below the northern face of the Kızılkaya Peak, there is a cirque bowl that is still active, and inside it "Şiringöl", which is a glacier lake.

There are different routes of varying degrees of difficulty for the ascent to the Kızılkaya Peak. Each mountaineer will determine his or her own route of ascent. For this, each mountaineer should first carry out a reconnaissance tour. A secure ascent to the Kızılkaya Peak (3771 m.) will begin at the campsite. The 3500 metre-high Kızılkaya ridge to the east of Kızılkaya will be climbed. The ascent will begin from there. To the east of this ridge there are two beds of "glacier nuclei". The glacier nuclei are partially buried.

Mountaineers who have reached the Kızılkaya ridge (3500 m.) will continue their ascent from there and reach the Kızılkaya Peak (3771 m.). The Kızılkaya ascent along this route will last around six hours. The return will not follow the same route. During the return, the south-western slope of the mountain will be followed until the "Çelikbuyduran" ridge and the upper part of the Yalak Valley, and then finally the campsite at the Yedigöller Valley are reached. Return to camp along this route will last around 3-4 hours.

Mountaineers proficient in the climbing technique with ropes and pegs can climb the Kızılkaya Mountains (3771 m.) also from the northern side. This side of the mountain has a solid face of rock. In this case too the descent will be made along the western side.

The Yedigöller Direktaş Ascent

The 3510 m.-high Direktaş Peak rises to the south-east of the campsite. Normal ascents of Direktaş are done from the southern face. The ascent will begin with a trek from the campsite. Following a trek of 20-30 minutes, the point to the south of the mountain, where the ascent to the peak begins, will be reached. The ascent will last around 3-4 hours and return to camp will follow the same route. Sufficiently capable mountaineers can carry out an ascent with ropes and pegs also on the northern face.

Aladağlar Passage "Trans-Taurus"

Mountaineers who have completed their excursions, studies and ascents at Yedigöller, can move on to Barazama "Ulupınar" via the "Hacer Pass", thus accomplishing a Trans-Taurus trek. The Yedigöller-Barazama trek will last around 5-6 hours. Mountaineers,who have completed the Aladağlar passage can proceed to Adana via the Barazama-Karsantı highway (around 120 km.) or go to Kayseri via Yahyalı.

Ascent Up Kaldı Mountain (3688 m.)

At the extreme south of the Aladağlar is the 3688 m.-high Kaldı Mountain. For a normal ascent up Kaldı Mountain, camp will be set up at Akşampınarı, while for ascents along the north, camp will be set at Sıyırma Pass "sulağankeler". The Kaldı Mountain ascent from the west will begin at the Akşampınarı campsite. The ascent will proceed towards the south until a place called "Avcıbeli" is reached. Following that, the ascent towards the east will continue until "Kaldıbaşı" and then Kaldı Peak (3688 m.) are reached. Return to camp will follow the same route. Ascent to the peak from this side and the return will last 8-10 hours. Technically difficult ascents to Kaldı Mountain are in general done along the north-eastern and northern ridges. The Sıyırma Pass will be used as a campsite.

Ascents to the Güzeller and Gürtepe Peaks

To the north-east and east of Emli Valley lie Cebel Mountain (3630 m.), Gürtepe (3474 m.) and Güzeller Peak (3461 m.). Mountaineers wishing to climb these peaks will set up camp at the Sulağankeler Plateau on Sıyırma Pass, which is at the end of Emli Valley. From this campsite, pleasurable ascents to peaks like Güzeller, Gürtepe, Cebel or Özgüdek (3620 m.) can be carried out. From this campsite it is also possible to pass on to the Turasan Mountains.

Ascents Up the Turasan Mountains

Ascents to Boruklu Peak (3548 m.) and to Vayvay Peak (3565 m.) on these mountains can begin from either Sıyırma Valley or Yedigöller Valley.

Mountaineers traveling over the Sıyırma Valley-Sulağankeler Plateau will set up camp at Kokorot Valley, while mountaineers proceeding along the Yedigöller Valley will set up camp at Karagöl Valley.

Those wishing to approach the Turasan Mountains from Adana will first climb to the Acıman (Tırak) Plateau via Karsantı-Kökez Village. The distance between Adana and Karsantı is 75 km., while that between Karsantı and the Acıman Plateau is around 40 km. The trek from Acıman (Tırak) Plateau to the Vayvay Tepe campsite will last 6-7 hours.

Mountaineers approaching from this direction will find dense forests and consequently a very varied fauna and natural scenery on the Mediterranean facing slopes of the Taurus Mountains.

Excursion and Ascent Programme

1st day: Çukurbağ-Sokulupınar.
2nd day: Demirkazık (3758 m.) ascent from Narpuz Valley.
3rd day: Excursion to the Çımbar Valley.
4th day: Sokulupınar-Yalak Valley-Yedigöller.
5th day: Rest at Yedigöller Valley (3100 m.).
6th day: Kızılkaya (3771 m.) ascent.
7th day: Direktaş ascent (3510 m.).
8th day: Yedigöller-Barazama or Yedigöller-Emli Valley.
9th day: Emli Valley-Akşampınarı.
10th day: Kaldı Mountain (3688 m.) ascent.
11th day: Akşampınarı-Sulağankeler.
12th day: Güzeller Mountain (3461 m.) ascent.
13th day: Cebelbaşı (3630 m.) or Özgüdek (3620 m.) Peak ascent.
14th day: Emli Valley-Çukurbağ Village.

Updated Information and Recommendations

The Taurus-Aladağlar or the village of Çukurbağ are reached by means of the Niğde-Çamardı highway (65 km.). This highway is paved with asphalt. There are regular bus trips between Niğde and Çamardı. Those who do not have a car can take one of the minibuses or buses which depart from the Niğde bus station for Çamardı once every hour.

The most suitable time for summer excursions and ascents up the Taurus-Aladağlar is late May and the months of June, July and August. February and March meanwhile are the most suitable time for winter excursions and ascents.

Teams carrying out summer ascents up the Taurus-Aladağlar will in general be advancing on rocky surfaces without snow. Excursion clothing and equipment should be chosen acccordingly. So as to be able to protect oneself against the sun rays, which are very strong in the area, light coloured cotton clothes should be preferred.

In addition to this, mountain boots with thick soles and leggings should be used so as be able to cross the many piles of pebbles (çarşak) with ease. Excursions and ascents on the Aladağlar should not be undertaken without a guide, as these mountains occupy a vast area. Mountaineers should have sleeping bags and mountain tents in sufficient number for all excursions and ascents up the Taurus-Aladağlar. At the village of Demirkazık there is a 60-bed "sports training centre" and an 81-bed mountain refuge. These facilities are open year-round.

In the summer, the Toros-Aladağlar are crowded with semi-nomadic Yörüks and migrant herders going to the highlands. The herds, which at night are taken to high pastures, are brought back to the plateaus in the morning for "milking". The meeting of lambs or "kuzukatımı" when the female sheep are brought to the plateau before the milking and meet the lambs on the plateau is worth seeing. As a natural extension of sheep raising, carpet and kilim weaving too is widespread in the villages of the area. Those wishing to do so can both see the weaving looms and buy carpets.

Mountaineers conducting the "Trans Taurus" trek and descending to the Barazama "Ulupınar" Village should be sure to see the waterfalls in the village of Karpuzbaşı.

For Further Details:

General Directorate of Youth and Sports
Turkish Mountaineering Federation
4th Floor, Ulus / ANKARA
Phone: 0(312) 311 91 20 - Fax: 0(312) 310 15 78
E-mail: tdf1966@hotmail.com
Website: www.tdf.org.tr

Demirkazık Mountaineering and Nature Sports Club
Bor Caddesi No:70/17, NİĞDE
Phone: 0(388) 232 15 08 - Fax: 0(388) 232 49 04
Website: www.treckinginturkeys.com
E-mail: sobek@keynet.net

Demirkazık Mountain Refuge
Demirkazık Köyü Çamardı, NİĞDE
Phone: 0(388) 724 72 00

KAYSERİ-MOUNT ERCİYES (3917 m.)

Mount Erciyes (3917 m.), which is among Turkey's important centres for mountaineering and winter sports, rises to the south of Kayseri Plain (1100 m.). To the west of the mountain is Sultansazlığı, and to the south the Develi Plain. Mount Erciyes, which is around 2900 metres higher than the surrounding plains, is the highest volcano of the Central Anatolia Area.

Mount Erciyes, the peak of which is covered year-round by snow and frozen snow, has the appearance of a high, majestic mountain. According to historical records, the name Erciyes or Erciyas derives from "Ercaş Bey", who was a Seljuk frontier principality lord. Mount Erciyes, which has a diameter of around 18 km. and a surface area of approximately 1000 km^2, is located at the north-eastern extremity of the Central Anatolian Series of Volcanoes. Mount Erciyes is an extinct volcano and has the characteristics both of a "layered volcano" and of a "pile volcano". It is for this reason that it has a geological and morphological structure of worldwide importance.

It seems that the first "mountain climbings" to Mount Erciyes were done by local young Christian priests. The "carved niche" at the summit area of Mount Erciyes, at an altitude of around 3850 metres, and the "cross sign" on the wall of this niche, confirm this to be the case. The first summer ascent along the north face of Mount Erciyes, which has been climbed many times during the last century by both Turkish and foreign mountaineers, was conducted on 23rd August 1973 by the Swiss mountaineer M. Wacker. The "first winter ascent" by Turkish mountaineers to the main peak of Mount Erciyes (3917 m.) was accomplished in March 1967.

The Formation of Mount Erciyes
"Geological Structure and Topography"

While the Tauruses, which are like a wall along the south of the Anatolian peninsula, and which are part of the Alpine-Himalayan Mountain Belt, were completing their formation during the Upper Tertiary Period, certain horizontal and vertical "tectonic movements" were happening in the Central Anatolian Area, which lies to the north of the Tauruses. These geological series, which in general are made up of hard-massif rocks and which are widespread in the Central Anatolia Region, were affected by these horizontal and vertical movements, resulting in violent breaking and vulcanism.

As a result of this violent vulcanism, which began in the Upper Tertiary and continued all through the Quaternary, the area has a Central Anatolian Volcano Series, which is set over an active 250 km.-long "fault line" beginning from the south of Konya and extending to Kayseri, and upon which are located the Karadağ (2288 m.), Karacadağ (1950 m.), Hasandağı (3268 m.), Melendiz Mountain (2963 m.) and Mount Erciyes (3917m.) volcanoes. The Erciyes Volcano is located at the north-eastern extremity of this series and is the highest volcano of the Central Anatolian Area.

Volcano Morphology of the Mount Erciyes

The Erciyes vulcanism has evolved in three main stages. These are:

Initial Stage of Vulcanism: During this stage, basaltic tuff series and consequently basaltic lava emerged through crevasse eruptions. These series that make up the base layers of the Erciyes Volcano occupy a vast space in the area.

Central Stage of Vulcanism: During this stage, volcanic rocks with andesite and andesite agglomerate alternation forming Mount Erciyes's central cone and body erupted. Following this stage, many parasitic conduits connected to the main channel gave Mount Erciyes its "cluster volcano" structure.

Late Stage of Vulcanism: During this stage, the main and secondary channels of Mount Erciyes were blocked, with the result that it acquired the nature of a volcano ejecting mainly pyroclastic materials (volcano pebbles, volcano sand and tuff) and piling them up faraway.

The 3917 metre-high Erciyes Volcano has been subjected to effective erosion by glaciers and frozen snow and also to external forces like freezing-melting phenomena. The crater of Erciyes Volcano, which was partially broken by the last eruptions, was totally destroyed by these external forces.

While the main crater was destroyed, the main cone of the volcano at the altitudes of 3000-3900 metres has maintained its general characteristics. This cone that gives the mountain its later "strato volcano" nature is made up of andesite agglomerate. This main cone has a very rough look, and on it there are frozen snow and glaciers.

Pyroclastic volcanic material (like volcanic tuff, volcanic ashes, volcanic sand, pumice), which was ejected by the Erciyes Volcano during the first and most violent eruptions of the Upper Miocene and Pliocene eras and spewed over distances as great as 100 km., sedimented in Neogene land or lake basins, forming geologic layers with a thickness of tens of metres. These series of tuff that surfaced when these lakes were drained through cracks or evaporation, were then broken by external forces like freezing-melting, surface sweeping and wind erosion, leading to the creation of that amazing volcanic topography called "fairy chimneys" seen in the environs of Ürgüp.

Glacier Morphology on Mount Erciyes

Mount Erciyes is among the places in Turkey where glacier morphology is present. On Mount Erciyes (3917 m.) you can see glacier topography of both the Ice Age, and of our times, side by side or even superimposed.

Vast, thick glaciers overflowing from feeding bowls during the Ice Age got embedded, especially on the north-eastern and north-western slopes of the mountain, and descended to altitudes as low as 2200 metres. The primary big glaciers that formed during that period were the Aksu Glacier on the NW slope of Mount Erciyes, and the Öksüzdere and Üçker glaciers on the NE and E slopes. These glaciers from the Würm (II) era disappeared as a result of rising temperatures and aridity, and in their places big vessel valleys "glacier valleys" appeared.[10]

Today on Mount Erciyes there is only a single glacier. This glacier, embedded on the NW slope of the mountain at an altitude of around 3400 metres, has a length of approximately 700m.

Water Conditions "Hydrology"

There are not many streams or lakes on the peaks and main body of the Erciyes Volcano, which is made up of volcanic layers like andesite and agglomerate that are porous and loose. During the summer, water from the melting of frozen snow and glaciers follows gravity and the incline to flows towards the bottoms of valleys and plains as "unconfined aquifers".

Underground water feeding off of the year-round snows on the peak of Mount Erciyes, surfaces at four locations. One of these locations is Tekir Plateau on the eastern side of the mountain at an altitude of 2150 metres. These underground waters provide a constant stream of water for the Seyfe Stream flowing between

---

10 Mountaineers ascending the E and NW slopes of Mount Erciyes will cross these ancient glacier valleys. This book's writer, İsmet ÜLKER, has himself crossed these valleys many times.

Koçdağı and Tekir Yaylası in the SN direction. The other sites where the waters of melting snow and frozen snow surface are Sultansazlığı to the west of the mountain, Karasazlık to the north-west, and Çayırözü to the south.

Natural Vegetation and Wildlife
"Flora and Fauna"

The northern slopes of Mount Erciyes (at altitudes of 1100-1600 metres) are completely covered with vineyards and orchards, while at the altitudes of 1600-2500 metres, we find mountain pastures. Higher up there are Alpine plants. Chief among the mountain flowers typical of Mount Erciyes are the "anemone ablana" known as Mountain Tulip or Tulip of the Caucasus, violet and white campanulae and wild orchids. The campanulae and orchids bloom in late July on Tekir Plateau while the Mountain Tulips bloom in May.

The high mountain meadows on the eastern, northern and western slopes of Mount Erciyes (at altitudes of 1600-2500 metres) are used all through the summer as highland settlements and pastures. Tekir Plateau on the eastern side of Mount Erciyes is an example of the mountain's famous highlands.

Among the wild animals present on Mount Erciyes, the most common are wolves and foxes. As for Sultansazlığı on the west of Mount Erciyes, it is an avian reserve of national and international importance. Hundreds of thousands of water fowl find a life-sustaining environment in this area.

Climatic Conditions and the Climbing Season

Mount Erciyes is located in Central Anatolia, which has a "steppe climate". In this climate, where summers are hot and dry, rains happen in winter and spring. Mount Erciyes, which is much higher than its surrounding area, receives its precipitations, and in particular its winter precipitations, primarily in the form of snowfall. There is still no meteorology station on Mount Erciyes. This is why we have indicated the meteorological data of Kayseri station on the table.

However, on Mount Erciyes there is a typical high mountain climate. There are big differences between daytime and nighttime temperatures. Air that gets extremely cold and heavy at night moves in a perpendicular direction, while air that heats up and expands in the day rises vertically. It is as a result of these movements that mountain and valley winds are formed.

The most suitable times for summer ascents on Mount Erciyes are June, July and August, while winter ascents are best conduction in the months of February and March. However, climbers have to be careful during horizontal and vertical air movements, snowfall, blizzards and foggy weather.

Name of the Station: Kayseri
Altitude: 1068 m.

	I	II	III	IV	V	VI	VII	VIII	IX	X	XI	XII	Yıl
Average monthly temperature (C°)	-2	0	4	11	15	19	23	22	17	11	6	1	11
Sunny and partially sunny days/month	19	18	19	22	26	28	31	31	29	27	22	20	290
Average number of snow-covered days/month	14	11	4	-	-	-	-	-	-	-	1	6	38
Greatest thickness of snow-cover (cm.)	28	35	21	12	-	-	-	-	-	-	42	25	42
Average monthly relative humidity	76	75	70	63	61	56	49	48	54	65	73	78	64

Source: Bulletin of the State General Directorate of Meteorological Affairs.

ASCENT UP ERCİYES MOUNTAIN

Two main routes are used for ascents up Mount Erciyes. Ascent up Mount Erciyes along the eastern face will begin at Tekir Plateau, while ascent up the north-western face will begin at Sütdonduran Plateau. The best to time to climb Mount Erciyes ıs in the months of June, July, August and September.

Mount Erciyes Ascent from Tekir Plateau

Tekir Plateau at an altitude of 2150 metres is also Mount Erciyes's winter sports centre. Tekir Plateau, located between Mount Erciyes and Koç Mountain (2628 m.), is at a distance of 25 km. from Kayseri and 12 km. from Hisarcık. The road is open year-round and is covered in cobblestones. On Tekir Plateau there is a 120-bed, two-star "mountain and ski refuge" with central heating and five two- or three-star hotels. The following is a list of lodging facilities on Mount Erciyes.

Grand Eras Hotel ****
Mount Erciyes, KAYSERİ
Phone: 0 (352) 342 21 28 - Fax: 0 (352) 342 21 38
erciyes@granderas.com - www.granderas.com

Mirada Del Monte ****
Mount Erciyes, Kayseri
Phone: 0 (352) 342 21 00 - Fax: 0 (352) 342 20 24

Mirada Del Lago ****
Mount Erciyes, KAYSERİ
Phone: 0 (352) 342 21 00 - Fax: 0 (352) 342 20 24

Ski Lodge ****
Mount Erciyes, KAYSERİ
Phone: 0 (352) 242 20 31 - Fax: 0 (352) 242 20 32

Ace Pension
Mount Erciyes, KAYSERİ
Phone: 0 (352) 342 20 53 - Fax: 0 (352) 342 20 56
info@aceerciyesotel.com

Bülent Hotel
Mount Erciyes, KAYSERİ
Phone: 0 (352) 342 20 12 - Fax: 0(352) 342 20 14
bulenthotel@hotmail.com – www.bulenthotel.com

The ascent up Mount Erciyes will begin at Tekir plateau. In three hours the Üçker glacier bowl will be reached. From the Üçker Bowl, mountaineers will climb to an altitude of around 3000 metres. The first camp will be set up at Çobanyurdu. From there the ascent can be done following one of two routes. The ascent up the peak will continue either along the Kuzuyatağı ridge to the south of the Üçker glacier bowl or along the "Şeytanderesi" valley to the west of the Üçker Bowl. During the trek in "Şeytanderesi", mountaineers should beware of rolling boulders.

The mountaineers climbing along these routes will first reach "Hörgüçkaya", followed by the eastern and then the western peaks. The trek from Tekir Plateau to the main peak will last around 6-8 hours.

ERCİYES MOUNTAIN MAP

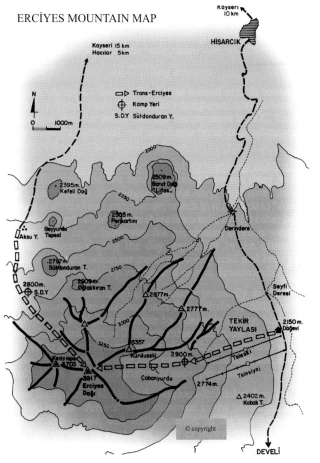

Ascent Along the North, Over Frozen Snow

Mountaineers wishing to climb to the peak along this slope will
go to Sütdonduran Plateau via Kayseri Hacılar - Aksuyurdu. The
Hacılar-Sütdonduran Plateau (around 20 km.) is a rough road
that can be used only in summer. This distance can be covered
on foot in 5-6 hours. Camp will be set up on Sütdonduran
Plateau (2800 m.), where there will be a day of rest and short
excursions.

On the second day, the mountaineers will begin their ascent to
the peak, and climbing along "frozen snow" embedded on the

north-western slope of the mountain, they will first reach the eastern peak of Erciyes (3891 m). And then, after having passed a ridge between the eastern and the western peaks, the

mountaineers will reach the bottom of the main peak (3917 m.). At that point, mountaineers will proceed to climb with the aid of rope up a seventeen (17) metre-high agglomerated block of rock and the ascent up the Mount Erciyes will be completed. Return to the campsite will be carried out along the southern slope of the mountain and along the main ridge. During the return, the ridge between Greater Erciyes and Lesser Erciyes "Ketintepe" will be reached. From there, return will be made to the campsite at Sütdonduran Plateau. This route is the shortest return route.

Sütdonduran - Tekir Plateau "Trans-Erciyes"

Mountaineers carrying out the Sütdonduran Plateau "northern frozen snow" ascent, can if they so wish do a "Trans-Erciyes" using the Eastern Peak-Hörgüçkaya-Şeytanderesi-Çobanyurdu route. It is recommended that mountain lovers wishing to do the Trans-Erciyes use Sütdonduran Plateau (2800 m.) as a starting point.

Ascent Programme

Ascent Along the Eastern Side
1st day: Kayseri-Hisarcık-Tekir Plateau
2nd day: Tekir Mountain Refuge-ascent up the Peak or camp at Çobanyurdu (2900 m.)
3rd day: Çobanyurdu-Şeytanderesi-Summit

Northern "Frozen Snow" Ascent
1st day: Kayseri-Hacılar Hacılar-Sütdonduran Plateau (2800 m.)
2nd day: Ascent up the peak or camp at Sütdonduran
3rd day: Sütdonduran-Tarakkaya-Eastern Peak, Western Peak (3917 m.)
The structure of the rock is not suitable for ascents with rope and pegs. It is for this reason that the "frozen snow surfaces" embedded on the east and north-east sides are recommended for summer and winter ascents. During winter ascents attention should be paid to horizontal and vertical air movements, and peak ascents should be avoided in cloudy and foggy conditions.

Summer and winter ascents of Mount Erciyess have different characteristics and degrees of difficulty. The most appropriate time for summer ascents is June, July and August, while for winter ascents it is February and March.

Updated Information and Recommendations

The Tekir Plateau mountain refuge is reached by taking the Develi minibuses departing from the Kayseri-Talas Garage every hour. Alternatively, one may take a bus to Hacılar from the bus station. A private vehicle is necessary to reach the Hacılar-Sütdonduran Plateau. The distance for Kayseri-Hisarcık-Tekir Plateau is 25 km.,while for Kayseri-Hacılar-Sütdonduran Plateau, it is 30 km.

During summer ascents, trekkers should take care to protect themselves from "sun stroke". Light-coloured cotton or woollen clothes are recommended. Those climbing to the peak should have with them mountain ropes, ice pickaxes and ice pegs. Ascents to the peak should be done with a guide.

On Tekir Plateau there are lodging facilities both owned by the state and by the private sector. Those climbing along the eastern face of Erciyes can use the "Tekir Plateau Mountain Refuge". Those climbing along the northern face must take tents and sleeping bags with them. On Sütdonduran Plateau there is also a recently built mountain cottage.

Mountaineers who have climbed Mount Erciyes should later visit the "Sultansazlığı" avian reserve and the world famous "Cappadocia Area". The life of the "Yörük", who in summer settle on the Mount Erciyes-Tekir Plateau, Aksu Yurdu and Serçer Plateau, and the "lamb meeting" repeated every morning are noteworthy spectacles of highland life.

For Further Details:

Turkish Mountaineering Federation
Youth and Sports General Directorate
4th floor, Ulus / ANKARA
Phone: 0 (312) 311 91 20 - Fax: 0 (312) 310 15 78
tdf1966@hotmail.com - www.tdf.org.tr

Hacılar Mountaineering and Winter Sports Club
Mayoralty Business Centre
Floor: 1, No: 9 Hacılar, KAYSERİ
Phone: 0 (352) 442 24 46 - Fax: 0 (352) 442 35 76
www.hadok.org.tr - hadok@hadok.org.tr

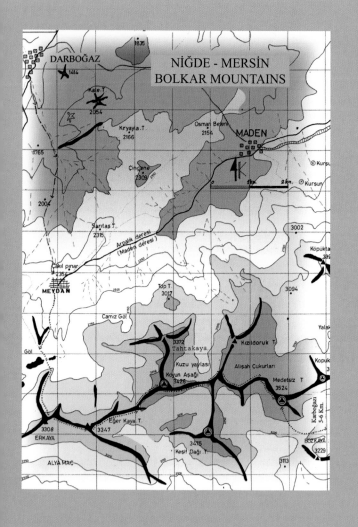

BOLKAR MOUNTAINS (3524 m.)

The Bolkar Mountains rising between the Göksu River to the west, and the Pozantı Çakıt Stream to the east, make up the second highest part of the Central Tauruses. The northern part of these mountains is located within Niğde province, while the southern part is situated within Mersin province.

These mountains in the Alpine-Himalayan fold mountain belt, have in general the nature of "napped" fold mountains. On these mountains made up of erodable stones like limestone and dolomite, there are elements not just of ancient glacier and stream topography, but also of "Karstic morphology".

Even though ancient glacier elements cover vast spaces on the Bolkar Mountains, there are no glaciers on them nowadays. Existing year-round frozen snow and snow areas are embedded on the northern slopes. Even though frozen snow erosion is strong in the higher regions of the Bolkar Mountains, and stream erosion strong in the lower parts, there is no visible or widespread web of streams on these mountains.

Since the main part of the Bolkar Mountains is made up of limestone and other similar porous rocks, rain water as well as the water of melting snow and frozen snow will seep underground without being able to be channelled on the surface. These waters that lead to a rich underground Karstic Hydrography in the Bolkar Mountains, surface as large "Karstic sources", such as Pozantı or "Şekerpınarı".

Medetsiz Peak (3524 m.), Keşifdağı (3475 m.), Koyunaşağı (3426 m.), Tahtakaya (3372 m.) and Eğerkaya (3347 m.) are the highest peaks of the Bolkar Mountains.

Ascent to the Medetsiz Peak (3524 m.)

The most appropriate ascents up the Medetsiz Mountain (3524 m.), which has the highest peak of the Bolkar Mountains, are those done along the northern and southern slopes. There are two routes to climb Medetsiz Peak.

Ascent over Darboğaz: The Darboğaz settlement, located at a distance of 9 km. from the Ulukışla-Pozantı highway, is connected to the main highway by an asphalt covered road. The distance between Darboğaz and Ulukışla is 22 km.

Following final preparations at Darboğaz, the campsite known as Meydan will be reached via the village of Emirler. This site is a flat highland with an average altitude of 2350 metres. To the south of this flat surface there are the lakes of "Karagöl" and "Çinigöl". Camp will be set up on Meydan Plateau or on the shores of Karagöl.

The distance between Darboğaz and Meydan is around 7 km. and the road is open in summer. The ascent up Medetsiz will begin at the campsite. Trekkers will first climb to the Koyunaşağı rising via the Erkaya-Eğerkaya ridges. From there, they will advance to Medetsiz Peak (3524 m.). Return to camp will follow the same route. The Medetsiz ascent, including return, will last 8-10 hours.[11]

Ascent Up Medetsiz Via Maden Village: For this ascent, trekkers will first have to climb to the village of Maden. The distance between Çiftehan Alihoca and Maden Village is around 25 km. After having progressed approximately 4 km. along the Maden-Meydan road, there will be a trek to Yalak Valley. Yalak Valley ends on the northern side of Medetsiz Peak. Camp will be set up at Yalak Valley at an altitude of around 2750 metres. The ascent to the peak will begin at the campsite. The ascent to Medetsiz (3524 m.) and return to campsite will last around 6-7 hours.

Ascent along the South Face: Those wishing to climb the Medetsiz Peak along its south face will first go by motor vehicle to Gülek. From Gülek they will go to the Karboğazı Plateau. This road, which is traveled by motor vehicle, is around 20 km. long. Mountaineers who have set up camp on Karboğazı Plateau (1900 m.) will first climb towards the west and then towards the north, and they will reach the summit of Medetsiz and return to the camp site on the same day.

MUNZUR MOUNTAINS (3462 m.)

The Munzur Mountains, which are the north-eastern extension of the Central Tauruses, are located in the provinces of Tunceli and Erzincan. The highest peak of this fold mountain range is that of Mercandağı-Akbaba (3462 m.).

Made of limestone rocks, the Munzur Mountains have a very rough topography with pointed peaks. The most suitable approaches for excursions and ascents up these mountains are Erzincan from the north, and Tunceli-Ovacık county from the south. There are air, land and rail connections with Erzincan, while Ovacık can be reached only by highway via Elazığ or Tunceli.

11 The Meydan and Karagöl area is very appropriate also for winter sports and it is an area with a high potential value.

The distance between Ovacık and Tunceli is 70 km. The highway follows the Munzur River to reach Ovacık. Along the highway there is the "Munzur Valley National Park". The fast running and limpid Munzur River is famous for its trouts and beautiful scenery.

Mountaineers planning to approach the Munzur Mountains from the south will first go to Ovacık via Elazığ-Tunceli. Ovacık is located in the central part of the Munzur mountain range and on the southern slopes of the Mercan Mountains. The highest peaks of the Munzur Mountains are those in the Mercan Mountains.

For the ascent up the Akbaba Peak (3462 m.), mountaineers will first enter Kırkmerdiven Valley through Ovacık-Şahverdi Village. After having set up camp at an appropriate location, the peak will be climbed. Following this, mountaineers might either do a "Trans Munzur" and go to Erzincan via Kılıçkaya, or they might return to Ovacık. Each mountaineer will determine the route and duration of ascent to the peak according to his or her own ability. To reach the camp site from Ovacık, mountaineers will have to rent pack animals and travel together with a local guide.

The most appropriate approach for an ascent to the Mercan Mountains-Akbaba Peak (3462 m.) from the north is Erzincan. After reaching Erzincan, mountaineers will go by motor vehicle to the village of Kılıçkaya (20 km.) via Çatalören. The Akbaba Peak (3462 m.) of the Mercan Mountains rises to the south-west of the village of Kılıçkaya. Mountaineers should first carry out a reconnaissance.

ANTALYA-BEYDAĞLARI (3070 m.)
"Olimpos and Kızlarsivrisi"

The Beydağları, which are the western part of the Taurus Mountains, are located within the borders of Antalya Province.

These mountains begin to rise to the west of the city of Antalya and extend towards the south. They comprise a veritable wall with a north-south extension along the coast of the Mediterranean.

There are many peaks on this mountain range. The main peaks are Tekedoruğu, Bakırlıdağ (2547 m.), Tahtalıdağ "Olimpos" 2360 m. and Kızlarsivrisi (3070 m.). Kızlarsivrisi (3070 m.) is the highest peak of this mountain range. These mountains, which in general are made up of limestone rocks, are covered with various kinds of forests. The high and majestic peaks of this mountain range rising along and above the Mediterranean coast, offer splendid, impressive scenery.

The highest peaks of these mountains are Tahtalı "Olimpos" Mountain, which can be reached via Kemer, and Kızlarsivrisi Mountain, which can be reached via Elmalı. The distance between Antalya and Kemer distance is 35 km., while that between Antalya and Elmalı is 125 km. The most interesting excursion and ascent in the Beydağları is that carried out on the Tahtalı "Olimpos" Mountain rising to the west of Kemer from the sea shore. This 2360 m. high mountain is covered in coniferous forests up to an altitude of 2000 metres, beyond which are mountain meadows.

For an ascent up Tahtalı mountain, mountaineers will first go by car from Kemer to Beycik Plateau (800 m.) on the south side of the mountain. It is from there that the ascent up Olimpos Mountain "Tahtalıdağı" begins. The ascent will be done from the south and along ridges with a view of the Mediterranean. The return will be done in part with a cable car reaching the village of Ağva.

The Kızlarsivrisi Mountain (3070 m.) will be approached by means of the Elmalı-Avlan Lake-Çamçukuru Plateau route (around 25 km.) and camp will be set up on Akoba Plateau (1750 m.). Any kind of vehicle is suitable to go there. It is located on the south-west slopes of the Kızlarsivrisi Peak.

Mountaineers who have set up camp on Akoba will climb the peak and return on the same day. The ascent to the peak does not present any difficulty. This area is very suitable also for winter Alpine skiing and touring skiing. The most suitable times for summer ascents consists are April, May and June. During these months, climatic conditions are temperate and moderate, and nature is in bloom.

MOUNT NEMRUT (3050 m.)

In Turkey, there are two Nemrut mountains. One is the Adıyaman-Mount Nemrut and the other is the Tatvan-Mount Nemrut. Both are of worldwide importance and fame; the first for archaeological, the second for geological reasons. What we are presenting now is the Tatvan-Mount Nemrut.

Tatvan-Mount Nemrut is a 3050 m.-high extinct volcano. This mountain, which lies in the province of Bitlis, rises above the south-western shores of Lake Van. To the south-east of Mount Nemrut there is the Tatvan county seat, and to the north the town of Ahlat.

Mount Nemrut, located at the extreme south of the Eastern Anatolia Series of Volcanoes, is the youngest of this series. According to Dr. Abich's findings, Mount Nemrut (3050 m.), which began to erupt during the Quaternary Period and continued its volcanic activities until 1441, has the characteristics of a "strato volcano". As a result of Mount Nemrut's volcanic eruption, the Van-Muş basin, previously a single basin, was subdivided into the Lake Van and Muş basins.

The Van Basin, which before the eruption of Nemrut Volcano was an open basin extending along a NS-SW axis, and the water of which was drained by the tributaries of the Murat River, became a closed basin when the lava coming out of Nemrut Volcano created a barrier extending along an east-west axis. By this means, Lake Van, which is a lava barrier lake with an altitude of 1720 metres and measuring 3765 km^2, was formed. Mount Nemrut's slopes and lower parts consist of basalt, the central parts of andesite, and the upper parts of volcanic glass.

On Mount Nemrut, which rises above the south-western shore of Lake Van, there is a "caldera" with a diameter of six km. and a depth of 650 metres. In Mount Nemrut's caldera bowl there are five lakes of various dimensions and a few parasitical volcano cones. To the north-east of the caldera bowl there are also two hot water sources. The caldera "crater" bowl has an altitude of 2400 metres.

Mount Nemrut attracts the attention of mountaineers and nature researchers all over the world, especially for its geological formation and the deep "caldera" on it. "Caldera" is a geological term of Italian origin meaning "cauldron".

Excursions and Ascent Up Mount Nemrut

The ascent up Mount Nemrut begins at Tatvan on the south-east slopes of the mountain. Following a normal trek of around 4-5 hours, mountaineers will reach either the southern or south-eastern edge of the Mount Nemrut "caldera". Mountaineers who have reached that point can see from up above the "cauldron bowl" of the Nemrut volcano. Mountain and nature researchers can reach Mount Nemrut's caldera bowl from Ahlat or Tatvan by means of an all-terrain vehicle.

Mount Nemrut is a barren mountain. To the south of the mountain there are tree clusters consisting of oaks (Quercus sp.) and birches (Betula sp.) (birches are sacred trees). The most suitable time for excursions and ascents to the Nemrut Caldera is June, July and August. Mountaineers climbing along the south-eastern and eastern sides will during the trek have a particularly spectacular view of the dazzling beauty, colours and scenery of Lake Van. Once over the south ridge, they will find themselves facing the extraordinary Caldera bowl.

DAPTATION TO WEATHER AND GROUND CONDITIONS ON MOUNTAINS

Mountaineering and winter sports activities have three important aspects, being "weather", "ground" and "social". One should never neglect the following general rules and principles so as to be able to carry out sports activities safely and adapt to the mountain environment both in summer and winter.

1. One should not go to the mountains during the transition seasons, on in other words, in early summer (April-May) or early winter (November-December). In these months, the weather will be unstable. They are also the months when avalanches and land slides happen most frequently.

2. In early winter, there are "breaking" avalanches and in late winter, "sliding" avalanches. This danger should be kept in mind and mountaineers or skiers active in these periods should avoid very steep, snow-covered slopes, and follow the bottom of valleys' "thalweg lines" where snow has settled.

3. When there are weather conditions characterised by cloudbursts, thunder and lightning, high ridges and pointed hills should be avoided. In such weather, metal equipment like pickaxes etc. should be kept at a distance of at least 20-30 m. from the tents of the camp.

4. During unfavourable weather conditions, ascents to peaks and other similar activities should be avoided, and at such times, precedence should be given to "acclimatisation" and rest.

5. For "winter ascents", which necessarily must be conducted in the 21st December - 23rd March period, dates between 20th January and 20th March should be preferred. In those days, weather conditions will be more stable, and snow-covered ground will offer a more secure climbing environment.

6. People taking part in mountaineering and skiing activities should dress to protect themselves from strong sun rays, both in summer and in winter. They should have appropriate goggles against snow blindness and should apply protective lotions as well.

7. In Turkey's ski centres, avalanches are not a very common phenomenon. There are avalanche creating bowls only on the northern slope of the Büyük Ejder Peak of Palandöken Mountain, and on the north-western slope of Uludağ. The danger of avalanches in these two areas is present only in the aftermath of considerable snowfall, when there is plenty of fresh snow.

Apart from this, whenever there is a thick fog on the Uludağ or Kartalkaya ski centres, skiers should not stray from ski runs.

8. For example, mountaineers climbing the Greater Ararat in winter along the southern face and following the normal route, should carry out a "rope aided secure passage" while traversing the Ülkeroğlu "Southern" Glacier. As for mountaineers doing a Trans-Kaçkar, they should have a local guide with them, due to the danger of fog.

INSTITUTIONS OFFERING SERVICES FOR MOUNTAIN EXCURSIONS IN TURKEY

Ministry of Culture and Tourism
General Directorate for Promotion
İnönü Bulvarı No: 5, Bahçelievler - ANKARA
Phone: 0(312) 213 17 85 - Fax: 0(312) 213 68 97
info@kultur.gov.tr

Turkish Mountaineering Federation
General Directorate for Youth and Sports
Floor: 4, Ulus - ANKARA
Phone: 0312 311 91 20 - Fax: 0312 310 15 78
www.tdf.org.tr - tdf1966@hotmail.com

TRAVEL AGENCIES ORGANISING MOUNTAIN EXCURSIONS

Ayder Tourism
İzmir Caddesi No: 13/1, Kızılay – ANKARA
Phone: 0(312) 232 42 33 - Fax:0(312) 232 42 34
www.ayder.com.tr ayder@ayder.com.tr

Tempo Tourism
Tunalı Hilmi Caddesi Binnaz Sokak No: 1/4
Kavaklıdere - ANKARA
Phone: 0(312) 428 20 96 - Fax: 0(312) 426 16 70
www.tempotour.com.tr

Bukla Tourism
İnebolu Sokak No:55/4
Setüstü - Kabataş - ISTANBUL
Phone: 0(212) 245 06 35 - Fax: 0(212) 245 08 14
www.bukla.com

Tamzara Tourism
Yeniçarşı Caddesi No: 36 K.4 No:5
Beyoğlu - ISTANBUL Phone: 0(212) 251 98 64
www.tamzaratur.com

Explorer Tourism
Cinnah Caddesi No:40/16
Çankaya - ANKARA
Phone: 0(312) 438 00 95 - Fax: 0(312) 438 00 96
www.explorer.com

Sobek Tourism
Bor Caddesi No:70/17
NİĞDE
Phone: 0(388) 232 15 07 - Fax: 0388 232 49 04
www.treckingturkeys.com www.sobek.keynet.net

Demavent Tourism
Esenbey Mahallesi Bağadır İş Merkezi, Kat: 2, No:5 NİĞDE
Phone: 0388 232 73 63
www.yellowpages.com

Türkü Tourism
İnönü Caddesi No:47, Çamlıhemşin - RİZE
Phone: 0464 651 72 30 - Fax: 0464 651 75 70
www.turkutour.com

MOUNTAINEERING CLUBS

Hacettepe University Mountaineering and Nature Sports Club
Beytepe - ANKARA
www.mountain.hacettepe.edu.tr

Orta Doğu Technical University Mountaineering and Nature
Sports Club
ODTÜ - ANKARA
www.metu.edu.tr

University of the Bosphorus Mountaineering Club
Ortaköy – ISTANBUL
www.budak.boun.edu.tr

Yıldız Technical University Mountaineering Club
Beşiktaş - ISTANBUL
www.ytudak.org.tr

University of the Mediterranean Mountaineering Club
Bahçelievler - ANTALYA
www.akdeniz.edu.tr

Hacılar Mountaineering and Winter Sports Club
Mayoralty Business Centre Kat: 1 No: 9
Hacılar - KAYSERİ
Phone: 0352 442 24 46 - Fax: 0352 442 35 76
www.hadak.org.tr

Demirkazık Mountaineering and Nature Sports Club
Bor Caddesi No: 70/17 , NİĞDE
Phone: 0388 232 25 08 - Fax: 0388 232 49 04
www.treckingturkeys.com

Eastern Black Sea Nature Sports Club
Eski Terminal Üstü, Ardeşen - RİZE
Phone: 0464 715 53 01 - Gsm: 0536 706 62 73
info@dokadak.com

İzmir Mountaineering and Nature Sports Club
1484 Sokak No: 3/1, Alsancak - İZMİR
Phone: 0232 421 30 10 - Fax: 0232 464 73 78
www.idadik.org.tr idadik@egenet.com.tr

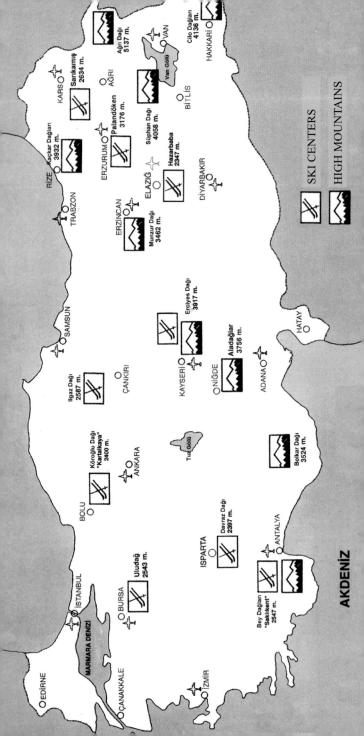

SKI CENTERS

HIGH MOUNTAINS

AKDENIZ

TURKEY'S WINTER SPORTS CENTERS

In this chapter, an attempt has been made to present and evaluate Turkey's existing ski centres of regional and national importance, and also those areas possessing great potential for usage as such. Particular importance has been attributed to the location and position of these centres and areas, to transport facilities, to the best seasons for skiing and snow conditions, to the description of skiing courses and finally, to the mechanical facilities serving the skiing trails.

The main features determining whether or not an area is appropriate for Alpine skiing have been the existence of slopes with regular surfaces, inclines of between 30% and 75%, a length of at least 1500 m. and a drop in height of at least 200 m. Identification of areas conducive to conducting competitions and freestyle skiing has been carried out with an eye to the rules and "threshold" values of the International Skiing Federation ("F.I.S.").

As for the determination of the "skier/day/carrying" capacity of ski areas, the "$100m^2$/area/one skier" parameter, or the ski area carrying capacity "SKCC" formula indicated below, have been used in their calculation.

For example, the "skier carrying capacity" of a ski piste can be found by multiplying length and width and dividing the result by "100", or by using the SKCC formula. ($100m^2$ is the area reserved for a skier.)

$$SKCC = \frac{\text{Carrying capacity of the facility / hours } \times \text{ height } \times \text{ time}}{4000}$$

In this way, it is possible to determine the "skier/day/carrying" capacity of ski areas, both on the basis of the characteristics of ski pistes, and on the basis of the carrying capacity of mechanical facilities.

Turkey's high mountains and important primary ski centres have been indicated in the relevant map.

BURSA - ULUDAĞ

The Uludağ Ski Centre is located on the northern slopes of the Uludağ Massif rising in the southern part of Bursa. The ski centre is located 36 km. from the city centre of Bursa. The connecting road is cobblestone covered in part with asphalt and since it goes mostly through forested areas, it offers a view of extremely attractive scenery and natural beauties. The Bursa-Uludağ Ski Centre is also connected to the city centre by means of a newly built 8.8 km. long "Gondola" cableway, with eight seats and a 1,800-person/hour carrying capacity.

A great part of Uludağ, the historical name of which was "Olympus", meaning "Mountain of the Gods", is covered by mixed and coniferous forests, with "Alpine meadows" above the altitude of 1800 m.

The Uludağ Massif, which is made up mostly of internal eruption rocks and layers, such as those of granite and syenite, presents in part a broken topography, while the skiing areas have a more regular surface and a flat topography.

The Uludağ Ski Centre, situated between the 1650-2543 m. altitude belt, is part of the "Uludağ National Park". The Uludağ Ski Centre is one of Turkey's most important six main ski centres, because of its conditions that are especially conducive to winter sports and tourism.

Skiing Season and Snow Situation

The Uludağ Massif, the Köroğlu Mountains and the Ilgaz Mountains are the elevations that first receive the cold and snowy air masses coming from the Balkans. This is why they receive a lot of snowfall. In normal winter conditions, the thickness of snow reaches 300 cm. in the months of February and March.

The most appropriate time for skiing on Uludağ, which has a "120/day/year" skiing season, is the period between the 15th of December and the 30th of March. According to the long-term data of the Uludağ meteorology station, days with snowfall are 66/day/year, and the period of snow cover is 134/day/year, while the thickest snow cover is on average 280 cm. Similar conditions exist also on the Bolu-Köroğlu and the Ilgaz Mountains.

The Uludağ Ski Centre on the Bursa-Uludağ Massif (2543 m.) consists of three main areas. These are, in order from west to east, and from lower to higher parts, the Sarıalan Plateau, the First Development Area and the Second Development area.

SARIALAN PLATEAU

The Sarıalan Plateau in the western part of the ski centre, consists entirely of a plateau with inter-forest clearings. These areas at an altitude of 1650 m. are extremely suitable for free style and competitive "Northern skiing" and "Tour skiing" in particular.

The Sarıalan Plateau, which, although a suitable settlement area for the Uludağ Ski Centre, has not been used in this way, is connected to the Bursa city centre by means of a 5 km. long varangel "cableway", and to the Bursa-Uludağ Ski Centre road by means of a 3 km. long secondary road. The distance between Sarıalan and the Uludağ Ski Centre is 8 km.

FIRST DEVELOPMENT AREA

The "First Development Area" located in the forest between Cennetkaya and Fatihtepe is a ski area used mostly for training and freestyle skiing. In this area, there are 15 teleski and 4 chairlift facilities used for training. The highest point of this area is Fatintepe with an altitude of 2050 m.

The first and thus oldest hotels of the Uludağ Ski Centre were established in this area. These first facilities were followed by other hotel investments. The most important and relevant mechanic facilities established in the First Development Area for training purposes have been indicated on the map.

The following are the rankings and addresses of the lodging facilities located in the area.

Lodging Facilities

Grand Yazıcı Hotel (****)
1.Gelişim Bölgesi Uludağ – Bursa
Phone: 0(224) 285 20 50 - Fax: 0(224) 285 20 48
sales@grandyazici.com.tr

Uslan Hotel (***)
1.Gelişim Bölgesi Uludağ-Bursa
Phone: 0 (224) 285 20 21 - Fax: 0 224 285 20 27
hotelakfen@superonline.com.tr

Mihrace (Ak) Hotel (**)
1.Gelişim Bölgesi Uludağ-Bursa
Phone: 0 224 285 20 09 - Fax: 0 224 285 20 32
akesport@superonline.com

Beceren Hotel (***)
1.Gelişim Bölgesi Uludağ-Bursa
Phone: 0(224) 285 21 11 - Fax: 0(224) 285 21 18
beceren@telmar.com.tr -www.beceren.com.tr

Genç Yazıcı Hotel (***)
1.Gelişim Bölgesi Uludağ-Bursa
Phone: 0(224) 285 20 40 – Fax: 0(224) 285 20 45
info@yazicihotel.com – www.yazicihotel.com

Aydın Yıldız Hotel (**)
1.Gelişim Bölgesi Uludağ-Bursa
Phone: 0(224) 285 21 40 – Fax: 0(224) 285 21 42
rezervasyon@aydinyildizhotel.com
www.aydinyildizhotel.com

Kervansaray Uludağ Hotel (**)
1.Gelişim Bölgesi Uludağ – Bursa
Phone: 0(224) 285 21 87 – Fax: 0(224) 285 21 93
uludag@kervansarayhotels.com – www.kervansarayhotels.com

Ergün Hotel "Oberj"
1.Gelişim Bölgesi Uludağ – Bursa
Phone: 0(224) 285 21 00 – Fax: 0(224) 285 21 02
www.ergunhotel.com – info@ergunhotel.com

Fahri Hotel "Oberj"
1.Gelişim Bölgesi Uludağ – Bursa
Phone: 0(224) 285 20 10 - Fax: 0(224) 285 20 18
info@fahrihotel.com - www.otelfahri.com

Kar Hotel "Oberj"
1.Gelişim Bölgesi Uludağ - Bursa
Phone: 0(224) 285 21 21
karotel@karotel.com

Ulukardeşler Hotel "Oberj"
1.Gelişim Bölgesi Uludağ - Bursa
Phone: 0(224) 285 21 36 – Fax: 0(224) 285 21 39
info@ulukardesler.com - www.ulukadesler.com

Alkoçlar Oteli
1.Gelişim Bölgesi Uludağ - Bursa

SECOND DEVELOPMENT AREA:

This part, which lies within the boundaries of the Uludağ National Park and the Uludağ Ski Centre, contains the Uludağ Ski Centre's most suitable areas for winter sports and winter tourism, in terms of the vastness of the ski areas, the length of the pistes, the inclines and the existence of sufficiently high slopes.

The Second Development Area located between Mandıra Valley (1750 m.), Fatintepe (2050 m.), Kuşaklıkaya (2232 m.), Uludağ Peak (2543 m.), Tabutkaya (2133 m.) and Kırkgözler (1750 m.)

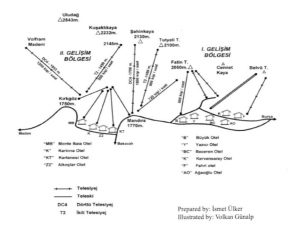

Prepared by: İsmet Ülker
Illustrated by: Volkan Günalp

has ski pistes suitable for Grand Slalom and Slalom competitions as certified by the F.I.S.

In this area, which is located within the boundaries of the National Park, there are five chairlifts, one teleski facility and five teleski facilities used for training purposes for new hotels. There are four hotels in the area as well.

The ski mechanic facilities in the Second Development Area have been indicated on the relevant map, while information about hotels is given below.

Lodging Facilities

Hotel Monte Baia (****)
2.Gelişim Bölgesi Uludağ - Bursa
Phone: 0(224) 285 23 83 – Fax: 0(224) 285 22 02
monte@baiahotels.com – www.baiahotels.com

Zone II Hotel (Alkoçlar) (**)**
2.Gelişim Bölgesi Uludağ – Bursa
Phone: 0(224) 285 22 88 – Fax: 0(224) 285 22 99
info@wowuludag.com – www.wowuludag.com

Otel Kartanesi (***)
2.Gelişim Bölgesi Uludağ – Bursa
Phone: 0(224) 285 24 30 – Fax: 0(224) 285 24 17
info@kartanesi.eu – www.kartanesi.eu

Karinna Hotel (***)
2.Gelişim Bölgesi Uludağ – Bursa
Phone: 0(224) 285 23 60 – Fax: 0(224) 285 23 61
info@karinnahotel.com – www.karinnahotel.com

Updated Information and Recommendations

The Uludağ Ski Centre is located 36 km. from Bursa, on the northern slopes of Uludağ, in the altitude belt of 1750-2543 m. It is possible to reach Uludağ from Bursa by private vehicles, taxis or the cableway. Fixed route taxis depart regularly from their stations near the new bus station and near the Ulucami Mosque.

Those wishing to go to Uludağ with their own cars should drive carefully, especially during foggy and snowy weather, and should have with them towing lines, a wooden wedge and tire chains. Especially in the case of those going to Uludağ for the first time, using the services of a travel agency will ensure a safe and comfortable trip.

Those travelling individually should reserve their beds before the trip. The most suitable period for skiing on Uludağ is 20th December – 30th March. In February and March, the thickness of snow generally reaches 300 cm. At the beginning of the season there will be "powder snow" and at the end of the season "wet snow".

Those just starting to ski should be trained by a teacher and should also rent equipment as recommended by the teacher. Undergoing two-hour per day, five-day training is very important if one is to have a safe skiing experience. Skiing equipment and clothing can be bought in the boutiques of the hotels of Uludağ.

In the Uludağ Ski Centre and especially during foggy and snowy weather, for the sake of personal security care should be taken not to leave the signed ski pistes and not to carry out excursions on skis in the forest without the supervision of a trainer.

There is a first aid station located on the mountain. In case of injuries sustained during skiing, specially organised units of the gendarmerie or ski trainers will carry out search and rescue services.

For Further Details:

Turkish Ski Federation
Türkocağı Cad. 29. Sk. No: 4/9, Balgat - ANKARA
Phone: 0(312) 285 11 38 Fax: 0(312) 285 11 32
www. kayak.org.tr – info@kayak.org.tr

Provincial Culture and Tourism Dirctorate
Osman Gazi Cad. No:6, Tophane - BURSA
Phone: 0(224) 220 99 26, Fax: 0(224) 220 42 51
www.bursaturizm.gov.tr

BOLU – KÖROĞLU MOUNTAIN

The Bolu-Köroğlu Mountain "Kartalkaya" Winter Sports and Tourism Centre, is located on the Köroğlu Mountain along the central part of the Istanbul-Ankara highway, within the province of Bolu. The Köroğlu Mountains, the lower parts of which are covered in pine forests and the upper parts in Alpine meadows, are mid-altitude (2400 m.) mountains receiving snowfall all through the winter. The Bolu Köroğlu Mountain Winter Sports Centre is located to the south-east of the city of Bolu, in the altitude belt of 1500-2400 m. and on the northern slopes of the Köroğlu Mountains. To the north of the Köroğlu Mountain "Kartalkaya" Ski Centre there is Sarıalan and the Kındıra Plateau, while to its south there is Kartalkaya (2221 m.) and the Köroğlu Peak (2400 m.).

This mountainous area, which has a natural environment suitable for winter sports and mountain and plateau climate cures, is one of Turkey's six main winter sports and tourism centres.

The northern slopes of the Bolu-Köroğlu Mountain are made up of rocks such as basalt, andesite and dasite, and are not rough. The widespread presence of permeable external ejection, andesite and dasite rocks leads to a stable ground preventing avalanches and land slides. This in turn provides for a secure and suitable location for ski trails and ski lodging facilities.

The ski areas are located between the altitudes of 1600 m. and 2400 m. Between 1600 m. and 1900 m. the ski trails are surrounded by pine forests of various kinds and by forest clearings. The higher parts at altitudes of 1900 m. – 2400 m. are devoid of forests, and are covered by Alpine meadows. There is no meteorology station at the Kartalkaya Ski Area.

Since the Köroğlu Mountains are the first obstacles encountered by precipitation-bearing air masses from the Balkans, they are among those areas in Turkey receiving the greatest amount of precipitation. In normal winters the Köroğlu Mountain ski areas have a "120day/year" ski season and in general by February and March their snow cover reaches 300 cm. The dominant winds of the area blow from the west and the north-west. However, when warmer southerly winds (lodos) blow in the winter, the snow may partially melt and become less suitable for skiing. According to on-site observations, in normal winter conditions, the most suitable time for skiing is 20th December – 10th April.

There are three ski areas on the northern slopes of the Köroğlu Mountains. These areas are, in order of importance, the

Kartalkaya, Köroğlu and Sarıalan ski centres. General and detailed information concerning these areas has been summarised below.

KARTALKAYA SKI AREA

"First Development Area"

The road leading from the Bolu-Ankara main highway, to the ski centre over Kındıra Village - Sarıalan Plateau is 28 km. long. At the Kartalkaya Ski Centre there are twelve ski mechanic facilities (three chairlifts, nine teleskis) and four hotels.

The ski areas of Kartalkaya are more suited to Alpine skiing and snowboarding and to freestyle skiing. The lodging and ski mechanic facilities and the ski pistes served by these facilities at the Kartalkaya Ski Centre have been indicated on the relevant maps, while the names and characteristics of lodging facilities are found below.

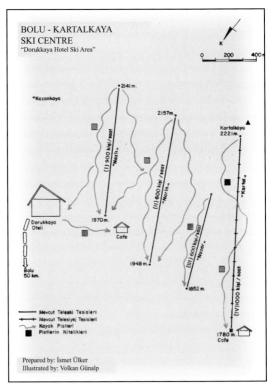

BOLU - KARTALKAYA SKI CENTRE
"Dorukkaya Hotel Ski Area"

Prepared by: İsmet Ülker
Illustrated by: Volkan Günalp

Lodging Facilities

As a result of planned development, the Kartalkaya Ski Centre has become one of Turkey's most important ski centres and it offers quality lodging facilities as well. The names, ranks, bed capacities and phone numbers of these establishments, all of which have Ministry of Tourism certificates, are indicated below.

Dorukkaya Oteli ***
"178 rooms – 482 beds"
Kartalkaya – Bolu
Phone: 0(374) 234 50 26 - Fax: 0(374) 234 50 25
dkinfo@kayatourism.com.tr – www.kayatourism.com

Grand Kartal ***
"131 rooms – 264 beds"
Kartalkaya - Bolu
Phone: 0(374) 234 50 50 - Fax: 0(374) 234 50 47
info@grandkartal.com -www.grandkartal.com

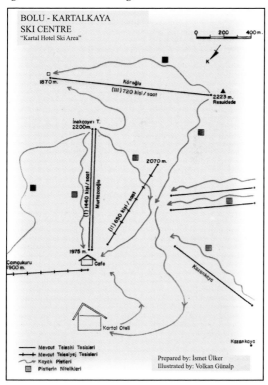

BOLU - KARTALKAYA SKI CENTRE
"Kartal Hotel Ski Area"

Prepared by: İsmet Ülker
Illustrated by: Volkan Günalp

Kartal Otel *
"163 rooms – 370 beds"
Kartalkaya - Bolu
Phone: 0(374) 234 50 05 - Fax: 0(374) 234 50 04
info@kartalhotel.com -www.kartalhotel.com

Golden Key Otel **
"72 rooms – 174 beds"
Kartalkaya – Bolu
Phone: 0(374) 234 50 80 - Fax: 0(374) 234 50 74
kartalkaya@goldenkey.com.tr www.goldenkey.com.tr

KÖROĞLU SKI AREAS

"Second Development Area"

The following proposals have been made for the Köroğlu Ski Centre, which, according to the Environmental Zoning and Construction Plan, has been deemed a "reserve resource area".

Following studies, the proposal has been made to establish two settlement areas and four mechanic facilities. The determination of the location of ski pistes has been carried out according to F.I.S. rules, and the ski area "skier/day/carrying" capacity has been calculated according to the "100 m²/area/one skier" parameter and the "SKCC" formula.

Around 2500 beds have been planned for this area, which is generally suitable for Alpine skiing, tour skiing, ski runs and snowboarding. The mechanic facilities planned for this ski area have been indicated in the relevant maps, while details regarding lodging establishments are indicated below.

The Köroğlu Ski Centre has been opened to new investments and planning has approved lodging projects, but these have not yet been carried out.

Establishment's Name - Rank (*)
Köroğlu Mountain R/A (*****)
Köroğlu Mountain R/B (****)
Köroğlu Mountain R/B1 (****)
Köroğlu Mountain R/C (****)
Köroğlu Mountain R/D (***)
Köroğlu Mountain R/E (***)

SARIALAN PLATEAU

"Third Development Area"

The Sarıalan Plateau within the Bolu-Köroğlu Mountain Winter Sports Centre, has an altitude of around 1600 m. and a diameter of 4 km., and consists of clearings within a forest. Sarıalan Plateau is particularly suited to ski races and tour skiing and also to climate cures and winter tourism activities; in addition, it has an environment and nature of rare beauty.

Updated Information and Recommendations

Those wishing to go to the Kartalkaya Ski Centre, which is located 50 km. from the Bolu city centre, and 28 km. from the Ankara-Istanbul highway, will follow the old state highway and at the 12th km. from the Bolu city centre, will leave the highway and go through the "Kındıra Village" to reach the Sarıalan Plateau and from there the Kartalkaya Ski Centre.

Those going by their own car in the winter should have with them tire chains, wooden wedges and tow ropes. Those wishing to go with a collective service rather than with their own car should organise their trip with the help of a travel agency.

The most suitable skiing season for the Kartalkaya Ski Centre is 20th December -30th March. At the Kartalkaya Ski Centre, which in normal winter conditions receives 300 cm. of snowfall, skiing is generally done on ground covered with "powder snow". On both Kartalkaya and the Sarıalan Plateau it is possible to do Alpine skiing, ski running and tour skiing.

Those wishing to go to ski centres with their own cars should reserve their places at the hotel. At the hotels of the Kartalkaya Ski Centre there are certified ski trainers. All sorts of ski equipment and ski clothing are available for sale in the boutiques of the hotels. Those who are just starting to ski should opt for rented equipment, the choice of equipment should be made under the advice of a trainer.

At the Kartalkaya Ski Centre, skiers should on no account leave the ski pistes in foggy or snowy weather and should not do excursions in the forest. Under normal circumstances, each hotel's first aid and rescue teams will intervene in case of injuries and similar accidents that may occur on the ski pistes. In addition to this, each hotel has health care units with trained personnel.

For Further Details:

Turkish Skiing Federation
Türkocağı Cad. 29. Sk. No: 4/9 Balgat - ANKARA
Phone: 0(312) 285 11 38 -- Fax: 0(312) 285 11 32
www. kayak.org.tr – info@kayak.org.tr

Culture and Tourism Directorate
Kültür Sitesi - BOLU
Phone: 0(374) 215 36 90 Fax: 0(374) 212 39 45
www.bolukulturturizm.gov.tr

KASTAMONU ILGAZ MOUNTAIN

The Ilgaz Mountains (2587 m.) rising within the boundaries of the Kastamonu and Çankırı provinces are similar in nature to the Uludağ and Köroğlu mountains. The Ilgaz Mountainous Area, being one of the first places to receive the cold and snow-laden air masses coming from the Balkans in the winter, receives a lot of snowfall throughout the winter.

The Ilgaz Mountains, the north facing slopes of which are generally covered with forests, are extremely suitable for winter sports and tourism, both because of their natural beauty and because of their snow-covered slopes. The Ilgaz Mountains, which have steep slopes that are particularly suitable for Alpine skiing, Nordic skiing, tour skiing and snowboarding, have a "120 day/year" ski season. The most suitable skiing season on the Ilgaz Mountains, where the snow cover surpasses 200 cm. in February and March, is that of 20th December – 30th March.

On the northern slopes of the Ilgaz Mountains there are three main areas suitable for winter sports and winter tourism. The first of these, the presently existing area which offers limited skiing opportunities, developed first and gained priority (because it is situated on the Ankara-Çankırı-Kastamonu main highway).

Of the other important areas, the second is located to the west of the existing Ilgaz Ski Centre, while the ski area with the highest potential and importance both at a regional and national level, is located on the "Çaklı Plateau" of the Great Ilgaz Mountain.

ILGAZ MOUNTAIN SKI CENTRE
"Existing Ski Centre"

The ski centre is located 4 km. to the west of the Çankırı-Kastamonu main highway, on the 1800-2000 m. altitude belt, within the boundaries of the "Ilgaz Mountain National Park". At the existing Ilgaz Mountain Ski Centre, which is located 200 km. from Ankara, 75 km. from Çankırı and 30 km. from Kastamonu, there are six lodging and two mechanic ski facilities.

One of the ski mechanic facilities is a chairlift, with a length of 1100 m. and a "1200 person/hour" carrying capacity. As for the other mechanic facility, it is a hanging "teleski" with a length of 1250 m. and a "1000 person/hour" carrying capacity.

Of the hotels within the existing Ilgaz Mountain Ski Centre, only the Doruk Otel and the Mountain Resort lodging establishments have Ministry of Tourism certificates. At the Doruk Otel and Mountain Resort establishments, which have a combined capacity of around 200 beds, there are certified ski trainers. As for the other hotels, they are boutique hotels with a 40-50 bed capacity each. The presently operating lodging establishments at the ski centre are indicated below.

Lodging Facilities

Ilgaz Mountain Resort (*****)
Ilgaz Kayak Merkezi – Kastamonu
Phone: 0(366) 239 10 40 – Fax: 0(366) 239 10 54
info@ilgazmountainresort.com
www.ilgazmountainresort.com

Ilgaz Dağbaşı Hotel
Ilgaz Kayak Merkezi – Kastamonu
Phone: 0(366) 239 10 10 – Fax: 0(366) 239 10 12
info@kayakturkiye.com – www.dagbasi.com

Ankara University Ilgaz Guest House
Ilgaz Kayak Merkezi - Kastamonu
Phone: 0(366) 239 10 61 - Fax: 0(366) 239 10 20

Ski Federation Ilgaz Mountain Hotel
Ilgaz Kayak Merkezi - Kastamonu
Phone: 0(366) 239 10 04 - Fax: 0(366) 239 10 06

Toprak Su Konukevi
Ilgaz Kayak Merkezi - Kastamonu
Phone: 0(366) 239 10 55

ILGAZ MOUNTAIN KUŞKAYASI SKI AREAS

Preliminary information about the "Kuşkayası Ski Areas" and the Büyük Ilgaz Mountain Ski Areas within the Ilgaz Mountains National Park, but outside the existing ski areas, which are more suitable for winter sports and tourism, has been summarised below. The Kuşkayası Ski Areas are located to the west of the existing ski centre, along the 1800-2042 m. altitude belt. It is believed that if the Kuşkayası Ski Areas between Kuşkayası, Bilovlar Peak (2042 m.) to its northwest and Yurduntepe (2333 m.) to its south, were to be opened to new investments, the existing Ilgaz Mountain Ski Centre would reach a carrying capacity of "2000 skiers/day".

GREATER ILGAZ MOUNTAIN
"Çaklı Plateau"

The Çaklı Plateau on the northern slopes of the Greater Ilgaz Mountain (2587 m.) is sufficiently steep, long and high for both

ILGAZ MOUNTAIN SKI CENTRE

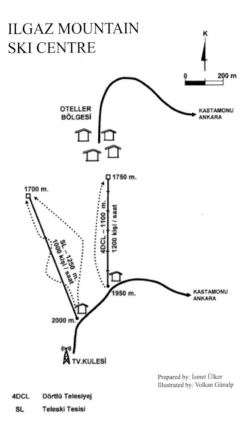

K

0   200 m

OTELLER
BÖLGESİ

KASTAMONU
ANKARA

1750 m.

1700 m.

SL – 1250 m.
1000 kişi / saat

4DCL – 1100 m.
1200 kişi / saat

1950 m.

KASTAMONU
ANKARA

2000 m.

TV.KULESİ

Prepared by: İsmet Ülker
Illustrated by: Volkan Günalp

4DCL	Dörtlü Telesiyej
SL	Teleski Tesisi

competitions and freestyle skiing according to F.I.S. rule and definitions, and has also a natural environment and forest beauty that are extremely suitable for both Alpine skiing competitions, ski runs and tour skiing. Following on-site research and evaluations, ski pistes and ski mechanic facilities to serve them, planned for the Greater Ilgaz Mountain-Çaklı Plateau Ski Areas, have been indicated on the map of the proposed master plan, and the characteristics and "carrying/hour capacities" of these facilities have been added.

The Greater Ilgaz Mountain-Çaklı Plateau Ski Areas located at the 1900-2587 m. altitude belt, have a total "2250 skier/day/carrying" capacity.

KASTAMONU - ILGAZDAĞI
SKI CENTRE "Big Ilgaz"

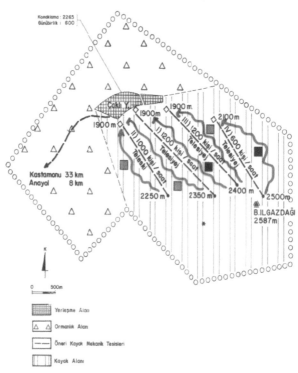

Prepared by: İsmet Ülker
Illustrated by: Volkan Günalp

For Further Details:

Turkish Ski Federation
Türkocağı Cad. 29. Sk. No:4/9
Balgat - ANKARA
Phone: 0(312) 285 11 38 Fax: 0(312) 285 11 32
www. kayak.org.tr - info@kayak.org.tr

Culture and Tourism Directorate
Cebrail Mah. 10 Aralık Cad. No:22
KASTAMONU
Phone: 0(366) 214 97 95 Fax: 0(366) 212 44 05
www.kastamonukulturturizm.gov.tr

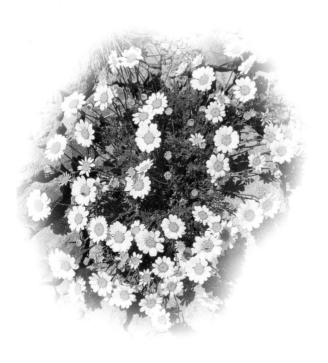

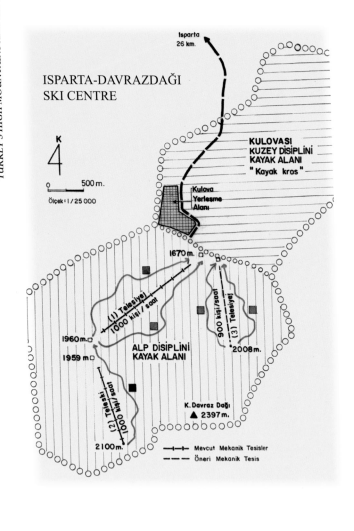

ISPARTA-DAVRAZDAĞI
SKI CENTRE

Isparta
26 km.

K
4

0 _____ 500 m.

Ölçek = 1 / 25 000

KULOVASI
KUZEY DİSİPLİNİ
KAYAK ALANI
" Kayak kros "

Kulova
Yerleşme
Alanı

1670 m.

(1) Teleşiyej
1000 kişi / saat

900 kişi/saat

(3) Teleşiyej

1960 m.

1959 m.

ALP DİSİPLİNİ
KAYAK ALANI

2008 m.

(2) Teleski
1000 kişi/saat

K. Davraz Dağı
▲ 2397 m.

2100 m.

├──┼──┤ Mevcut Mekanik Tesisler

─ ─ ─ Öneri Mekanik Tesis

ISPARTA – DAVRAZ MOUNTAIN

The "Davraz Mountain Ski Areas" are located on the north and north-west slopes of Davraz Mountain (2635 m.), at the 1600-2200 m. altitude belt, and at a distance of 26 km. from Isparta. This ski centre and its environs on Davraz Mountain to the south of Eğirdir Lake has a very particular natural environment.

The Davraz Mountain Ski Areas were first studied in March, 1994. These planning activities initiated by the Governor of Isparta at the time, Ertuğrul Dokuzoğlu, began to be put in practice according to the "Davraz Mountain Master Plan" prepared by İsmet Ülker, the writer of this book.

The Davraz Mountain Ski Areas have an environment suitable for Alpine skiing, Nordic skiing, tour skiing and paragliding. Kulovası, at an average altitude of 1650 m., is suitable for ski runs, while the slopes of varied nature, steepness and height on the northern slopes of the Lesser Davraz Mountain, at altitudes of 1650-2200 m., are suitable for Alpine skiing.

The north-eastern slopes of Davraz Mountain have ski pistes suitable for competitions and freestyle skiing according to F.I.S. rule and definitions; in normal winter conditions, its lower parts receive 50-100 cm. of snowfall, and its upper parts 100-150 cm. They have a "110 day/year" ski season during the 20th December – 10th April period. In the ski centre there are two chairlift facilities and one teleski, and a "ski refuge" with sixty beds and a 150-seat cafeteria. The two chairlifts have lengths of 1211 m. and 936m. and capacities of 1000 person/hour and 800 person/hour respectively, while the teleski has a capacity of 800 person/hour. The ski mechanic facilities at the Davraz Mountain Ski Centre and their characteristics have been indicated on the map, while existing lodging facilities have been listed below.

Lodging Facilities

Sirene Davraz Hotel ****
Davraz Dağı Kayak Merkezi / Isparta
Phone: 0(246) 267 20 02 – Fax: 0(246) 267 20 40
www.sirene.com.tr -davras@sirene.com.tr

Süleyman Demirel University Practice Hotel ***
Davraz Dağı Kayak Merkezi / Isparta
Phone: 0(246) 267 20 44 - Fax: 0(246) 267 20 42

Isperia Davraz Hotel (Oberj)
Davraz Dağı Kayak Merkezi / Isparta
Phone: 0(246) 267 20 20 - Fax: 0(246) 267 20 26
www.isperiahotels.com -mail@isperiahotels.com

Davraz Evleri Pansion
Çobanisa Köyü, Isparta
Phone: 0(246) 264 20 22 - Fax: 0(246) 349 64 53
www.davrasevleri.com -info@davrasevleri.com

New lodging facility investments are expected both on the
Antalya Belek coast, and in the Davraz Mountain Ski Centre,
which attracts people from big metropolises like Ankara and
İzmir. It is also possible to organise daily excursions to the
Davraz Mountain while staying in one of the hotels in Isparta
or Eğirdir.

For Further Details:

Turkish Ski Federation
Türkocağı Cad. 29. Sk. No:4/9
Balgat – Ankara
Phone: 0(312) 285 11 38 Fax: 0(312) 285 11 32
www. kayak.org.tr – info@kayak.org.tr

Culture and Tourism Directorate
Isparta
Phone: 0(246) 232 57 71
www.ispartakulturturizm.gov.tr

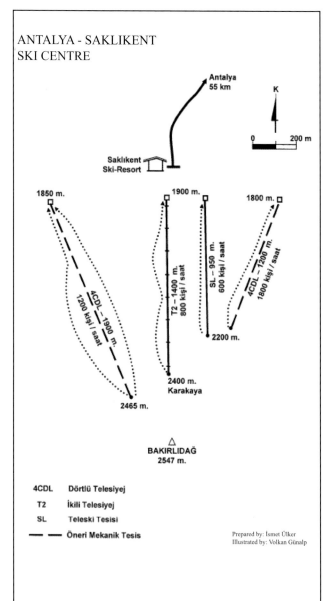

ANTALYA - SAKLIKENT
SKI CENTRE

Antalya
55 km

K

0   200 m

Saklıkent
Ski-Resort

1850 m.

1900 m.

1800 m.

4CDL – 1900 m.
1200 kişi / saat

T2 – 1400 m.
800 kişi / saat

SL – 950 m.
600 kişi / saat

4CDL – 1200 m.
1800 kişi / saat

2465 m.

2400 m.
Karakaya

2200 m.

△
BAKIRLIDAĞ
2547 m.

4CDL	Dörtlü Telesiyej
T2	İkili Telesiyej
SL	Teleski Tesisi
— —	Öneri Mekanik Tesis

Prepared by: İsmet Ülker
Illustrated by: Volkan Günalp

ANTALYA - SAKLIKENT

The Antalya-Saklıkent Ski Centre is located amongst the Antalya -Western Tauruses, on the northern slopes of the Beydağları-Bakırlıdağ (2547 m.). The Saklıkent Ski Centre is located at an altitude of 1800-2547 m. on the second line of heights on the land side of the Beydağları, which are parallel to the Mediterranean and extend along a south-north axis. It is a developing tourism and winter sports centre suitable for advanced skiing activities.

The Saklıkent Ski Centre, which is connected to Antalya by means of a 50 km. long asphalt road, was planned also as a "highland settlement". The last 9 km. of the highway are of compressed earth to make it easier to clear the snow. The Antalya-Saklıkent highway, which in places offers impressive scenery, remains open throughout the winter.

The Saklıkent Ski Centre is located within the transition belt between a temperate marine climate and a continental climate, and is closed to the Mediterranean's direct temperate effect, and in normal winter conditions gets around 100 cm. of snow. Depending upon winter conditions, in some years the lower parts get 50 cm. while the upper parts get up to 150 cm. of snow. The skiing season may be longer or shorter depending on winter weather conditions. The Antalya-Saklıkent Ski Areas, where in normal winter conditions the winter sports season lasts between 20th December and 30th March, has a "100day/year" skiing season. It is suitable most of all for Alpine skiing but also for activities like skiing races, tour skiing and paragliding.

The Alpine discipline ski pistes at the 1800-2547 m. altitude belt are up to international and olympic standards, both for freestyle skiing and F.I.S. competitions (especially because of the pistes' lengths, inclines and differences in height). Ski areas have a regular ground of limestone, covered with pastures. At Saklıkent, which was planned and developed as a ski centre and a "highland settlement", 500 lodgings for rent, a 70-bed motel and a guesthouse have been built. The motel contains a 300-person cafeteria and a 200-person restaurant. In addition, a 100-room, 300-bed, 3-star hotel is currently under construction. The only establishment presently in operation has been indicated below.

Saklıkent Ski Resort
Saklıkent Kayak Merkezi
Antalya
Phone: 0(242) 446 11 36-38 - Fax: 0(242) 312 66 56
www.skiresort.com – www.saklikent.com.tr

Ski Mechanic Facilities

The centre's Alpine ski pistes are served by a 1400 m. long chairlift with a 800 person/hour carrying capacity, two teleski facilities with lengths of 950 m. and 650 m. The Saklıkent Ski Centre has been indicated on the map of ski mechanic facilities serving the Alpine ski areas. Saklıkent, at a distance of 50 km. from Antalya, and within the 1800-2547 m. altitude belt, has a distinguished importance and attractiveness within Antalya tourism, thanks to its double identity of ski centre and "highland settlement".

For Further Details:

Culture and Tourism Directorate
Anafartalar Cad. No:31 , ANTALYA
Phone: 0(242) 247 76 60 Fax: 0(242) 248 78 70
antalya@kulturturizm.gov.tr
www.saklikent.com.tr – info@saklikent.com.tr

KAYSERİ – ERCİYES MOUNTAIN

Mount Erciyes (3917 m.) is not just Central Anatolia's highest mountain, but it is also very important as a centre of mountain sports and tourism. The Erciyes Volcano, rising to the south of the city of Kayseri, is an interesting mountain from the point of view of its geological and morphological structure. Mount Erciyes can be defined a "pile volcano" and a "layered volcano".

Mount Erciyes's volcanic eruptions ended in the early Quaternry and nowadays as an extinct volcano its crater has been broken especially as a result of glacier erosion, its slopes are covered with basaltic and andesite stones, and its topography is in places flat and regular, while in other places it is very rough and broken.

The Beyyurdu and Serçer plateaus in the north part of the Mount Erciyes and the Tekir Plateau on the east side of the mountain, consist in general of slopes with regular surfaces and various inclinations. These plateaus covered with pastures, receive a lot of snow all through winter, and are thus very suitable for winter sports.

Tekir Plateau on the eastern side of Mount Erciyes, within the 2150-3000 m. altitude belt, has nowadays become an important ski centre. The ski centre is at a distance of 25 km. from Kayseri over Hisarcık and of 12 km. from the Hisarcık settlement.

Since Mount Erciyes is one of Turkey's six most important ski centres and since this mountain is important also for mountaineering activities, the Derindere and Serçer plateaus have been taken up as a potential venue for a winter olympic and investments have begun.

Snow Conditions and the Ski Season

Mount Erciyes, which is located within the scope of the Central Anatolian continental climate, receives a lot of snow all through the winter. The Tekir Plateau, and the Derindere and Serçer plateaus, which in normal winter conditions receive 50-100 cm. of snow in their lower parts, and 100-150 cm. in their mid and higher parts, have ski areas and pistes up to F.I.S standards, and as such are suitable especially for Alpine skiing, Tour skiing, ski races and paragliding.

The most suitable time for skiing on Mount Erciyes - Tekir Plateau, which in normal winter conditions has a "150 day/year" ski season, is the 15th December – 15th April period. Depending of how the winter went, this period may extend up to May. There is no Mount Erciyes - Tekir Plateau meteorology station. It is for this reason that the following table contains the climatic data concerning the Kayseri meteorology station.

Name of the Station: Kayseri
Altitude: 1068m.

	I	II	III	IV	V	VI	VII	VIII	IX	X	XI	XII	Yıl
Average monthly temperature (C°)	-2	0	4	11	15	19	23	22	17	11	6	1	11
Sunny and partially sunny days/month	19	18	19	22	26	28	31	31	29	27	22	20	290
Average number of snow-covered days/month	14	11	4	-	-	-	-	-	-	-	1	6	38
Greatest thickness of snow-cover (cm.)	28	35	21	12	-	-	-	-	-	-	42	25	42
Average monthly relative humidity	76	75	70	63	61	56	49	48	54	65	73	78	64

Source: Bulletin of the State Meteorology Affairs General Directorate

Mount Erciyes Ski Areas

Tekir Plateau (2150 - 3200 m.) on the eastern slopes of Erciyes Volcano (3917 m.), the Derindere Area (1800 - 3350 m.) on its north-east slopes, Serçer Plateau (2100 – 2950 m.) on its northern slopes, have been organised as pistes suitable for Alpine skiing competitions and freestyle skiing, according to F.I.S rules and principles, while the lower part of Derindere has been reserved for Nordic skiing activities. The "Kayseri Mount Erciyes Ski Areas", for which there is a wish and plan to turn them into a winter olympics venue, are being equipped with advanced technology ski mechanic facilities (teleski, chairlift, telecabin).

The characteristics of the ski mechanic facilities planned for the Mount Erciyes Tekir Plateau, Derindere and Serçer Plateau ski areas have been indicated below the existing 8 chairlifts and 3 teleski facilities have been put into operation.

Of the new mechanic facilities the eight seat "8MGD" telecabin has a capacity of 2400 person/hour, the six seat "6CLD" chairlift of 2800 person/hour, of the other 4 four seat "4CLD" chairlifts one has a 2800 person/hour carrying capacity, and the others a 2000 person/hour.

Ski Mechanic Facilities

NAME	TYPE	LENGTH	UP-DOWN	GG	DIFFERENCE IN HEIGHT
A	SL	1432	2215	2460	245
B	CLF	1587	2205	2425	220
C	CLF	1563	2410	2770	360
D	SL	1518	2450	2740	290
E	SL	1414	2195	2445	250
F	8MGD	2150	2088	2636	548
G	6CLD	2250	2427	2939	512
H	4CLD	1540	2266	2605	339
I	4CLF	883	2440	2636	196
J	4CLF	1365	2429	2595	166
K	4CLD	1800	2267	2595	328
L	6CLD	2241	2430	3046	616
P	6CLD	2708	2270	2980	710
R	4CLD	1968	2865	3360	495

Updated Information and Recommendations

The ski areas being developed on Mount Erciyes -Tekir Plateau, Derindere and Serçer Plateau are all to the south of Kayseri on Mount Erciyes's north-eastern and eastern slopes (2100-3300 m.).

The ski centre is at a distance of 25 km. from Kayseri and of 12 km. from the settlement of Hisarcık. Kayseri is run by a metropolitan municipality and is connected to air, land and rail transport webs.

The Tekir Ski Centre can be reached by means of the "Develi" fixed route taxi service. The "Develi minibuses" leaving every hour from the Kayseri – Talas stop, go through Hisarcık and the Tekir Plateau.

Those wishing to go to the Tekir Plateau with their car in the winter will have to take with them tyre chains. The Kayseri-Tekir Plateau "ski centre" distance can be covered in around 30 minutes with a motor vehicle. It is recommended that in weather with snow, blizzard or fog those going to Tekir Plateau should

KAYSERİ - ERCİYES
SKI CENTRE

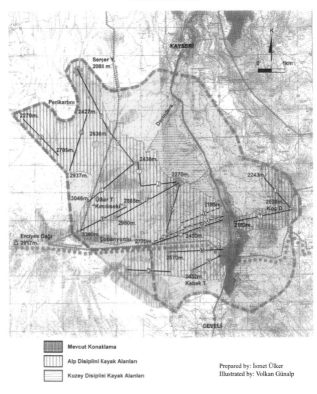

Mevcut Konaklama

Alp Disiplini Kayak Alanları

Kuzey Disiplisi Kayak Alanları

Prepared by: İsmet Ülker
Illustrated by: Volkan Günalp

be careful or wait for the weather to clear. In a similar way, one should not ski during foggy weather or when there is a blizzard, opting for a rest instead.

On Mount Erciyes the most suitable time for summer mountaineering activities consists of June, July and August, while for skiing activities it is the 20th December – 20th April. On Mount Erciyes, there is "powder snow" all through the ski season, and while in its lower parts the thickness of snow reaches 50-100 cm., in its higher parts it reaches 150-200 cm.

The lower parts of the Tekir Plateau, Derindere and Serçer Plateau have inclines of 15-30 %, its central parts of 30-45 % and its higher parts of 45-60 %. On the Tekir Plateau ski areas, all pistes, and especially the Büyükkapılı and Küçükkapılı pistes, are FIS certified.

There is the possibility of buying or renting equipment at the ski centre. However, it is advisable that the choice of rented equipment should be done under the supervision of the trainer. On the mountain there are certified ski trainers.

In the Kayseri - Erciyes Ski Centre there are lodging establishments of sufficient quality and capacity. There is also the possibility of using the hotels in the city centre in case of daily excursions.

The nature and addresses of the other hotels in the Mount Erciyes Ski Centre apart from the 120 bed Mountain and Ski refuge have been indicated below.

Lodging Establishments

Grand Eras Hotel **** Erciyes Dağı, KAYSERİ
Phone: 0(352) 342 21 28 – Fax: 0(352) 342 21 38
Erciyes@granderas.com – www.granderas.com

Mirada Del Monte ****
Erciyes Dağı KAYSERİ
Phone: 0(352) 342 21 00 – Fax: 0(352) 342 20 24

Mirada Del Lago **** Erciyes Dağı, KAYSERİ
Phone: 0(352) 342 21 00 – Fax: 0(352) 342 20 24

Ski Lodge ****
Erciyes Dağı, KAYSERİ
Phone: 0(352) 242 20 31 –Fax: 0(352) 242 20 32

Ace Pension
Erciyes Dağı, KAYSERİ
Phone: 0(352) 342 20 53 – Fax: 0(352) 342 20 56
info@aceerciyesotel.com

Bülent Hotel
Erciyes Dağı, KAYSERİ
Phone: 0(352) 342 20 12 - Fax: 0(352) 342 20 14
bulenthotel@hotmail.com – www.bulenthotel.com

For Further Details:

Turkish Ski Federation Türkocağı Cad. 29. Sk. No:4/9
Balgat - ANKARA
Phone: 0(312) 285 11 38 Fax: 0(312) 285 11 32
www. kayak.org.tr – info@kayak.org.tr

Mount Erciyes and Ski Refuge, Erciyes Dağı / KAYSERİ
Phone: 0(352) 342 20 31 Fax: 0(352) 342 20 32

ERZURUM - PALANDÖKEN

The Palandöken Mountain "Hınısboğazı" Ski Centre is located to the south of Erzurum, at a distance of 5 km. from this city, while the Konaklı Ski Centre is located at a distance of 18 km. from Erzurum, on the north and north-western slopes of the Palandöken Mountains. The Palandöken Mountains, which extend along a NE–SW axis, cover an area with a length of around 70 km. and a width of 30 km. The ski areas, which are located within the 2200-3176 m. altitude belt and run from north to south, are located in the Namlıkar, Hınısboğazı, Konaklı, Ülkeroğlu and Yağmurcuk areas.

The "Greater Ejder Peak" (3176 m.), which is the highest point of the Palandöken Mountains, and the "Lesser Ejder Peak" (3095 m.), rise to the south of the city of Erzurum and on the south border of the Hınısboğazı Ski Area.

The Palandöken Mountains were formed as a result of a vulcanism that began in the Tertiary Period and continued until the mid Quaternary Period, and that affected Eastern Anatolia. The Palandöken Mountains were formed by local "surface eruptions" along cracks on the surface, and in general are made of externally ejected andesite and dasite rocks.

This lava, which has a mid-level viscosity, on the one hand gained height, and on the other expanded horizontally, becoming thus a volcanic plateau with a length of around 70 km., a width of 25 km. and an altitude of 3176 m. As a result of the geological structure, the Palandöken Mountains do not have a rough or broken topography, but have long declines of various degrees, and as such are suitable for Alpine freestyle skiing and "olympic" competitions.

Snow Conditions and the Skiing Season

The Palandöken Mountains, which are a mountain chain of medium height, are in general covered with meadows and pastures. As a result, they are home to rich biological diversity in the summer.

The slopes covered with meadows and pastures make it possible for even the first snow of the winter to take a firm grip, thus making skiing possible even when there is a snow cover of only 20 cm.

Since there is no meteorology station on the Palandöken Mountains, data from the Erzurum meteorology station is provided below.

Name of the Station: Erzurum
Altitude: 1869 m.

	I	II	III	IV	V	VI	VII	VIII	IX	X	XI	XII	Yıl
Average monthly temperature (C°)	-8	-7	-3	5	11	15	19	19	15	9	2	-5	6
Sunny and partially sunny days/month	18	16	19	20	24	27	30	30	29	26	21	19	280
Average number of snow-covered days/month	29	26	24	5	-	-	-	-	-	1	5	23	114
Greatest thickness of snow-cover (cm.)	63	78	77	54	5	-	-	-	8	18	34	58	78
Average monthly relative humidity	76	75	74	65	60	56	50	46	49	60	71	75	63

Source: Bulletin of the State Meteorology Affairs General Directorate Note: The highest level of snow reached in the Erzurum city centre in the last 70 years was 135 cm. on 23rd February 2004.

As you can see from the climate data table, the highest level of snow in the Erzurum city centre is on average 78 cm., while the duration of the snow-cover season is 114 days. As a result of continental climatic conditions, it is possible to ski on "powder snow"-covered ski pistes all through the season.

However, ski areas on the slopes of the Palandöken Mountains that face the north, are higher than Erzurum and lie within the 2200-3176 m. altitude belt, and consequently have more snow that lasts longer.

According to observations in the area, the ski season is "150/ day/year", and includes the months of December, January, February, March and April. It has been observed that in normal winter conditions the snow cover on the ski areas is 50 cm. in the lower parts and 150 - 200 cm. in the mid and upper parts.

The Erzurum Palandöken Ski Centre, which is among Turkey's most important winter sports and tourism centres, was included for the first time in a planning activity in 1976 by the Ministry of Tourism, and for a second time in 1989 by the State Planning Organisation, when the cooperation of the Turkish Ski Federation, the Office of the Governor of Erzurum and the Erzurum Ski Club was sought.

Both planning activities were initiated and managed by İsmet Ülker, the writer of this book.

As a result of these planning activities, the "Hınısboğazı Ski Centre" on the Palandöken Mountains was appointed First

Development Area, while the "Konaklı Ski Centre" was appointed Second Development Area, and investments were directed accordingly. The location of the ski areas and pistes in both ski centres was determined on the basis of F.I.S. rules and parameters. In the case of pistes for competitions, the lengths of the pistes, the variety in inclinations and the differences in altitude were taken into consideration; in the case of freestyle skiing on the other hand, matters like the length and width of pistes and inclination were given precedence. For example, care was taken to ensure that pistes conformed to the "1 skier/100m²" area parameter and 1 to 10 proportion between the width and length.

HINISBOĞAZI SKI CENTRE

"First Development Area"

The "Hınısboğazı Ski Centre" is located at the 2200–3176 m. altitude belt, at a distance of 5 km. from the Erzurum city centre, and is particularly suitable for Alpine skiing competitions and freestyle skiing.

At the Hınısboğazı Ski Centre, there is one mountain and ski refuge, one ski training centre, and four good quality lodging establishments.

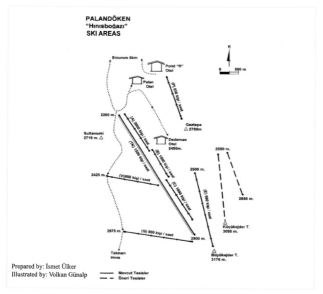

Prepared by: İsmet Ülker
Illustrated by: Volkan Günalp

Lodging Establishments

Dedeman Otel ****
Palandöken Kayak Merkezi, ERZURUM
Phone: 0(442) 316 24 14 - Fax: 0(442) 316 36 07
www.dedeman.com - palandoken@dedeman.com

Dedeman "Oberj"
Palandöken Kayak Merkezi, ERZURUM
Phone: 0(442) 317 05 00 - Fax: 0(442) 317 05 04
skilodge@dedeman.com

Polat "R" Otel *****
Palandöken Kayak Merkezi
ERZURUM
Phone: 0(442) 232 00 10 - Fax: 0(442) 232 00 90
palandoken@polatholding.com
www.polatrenaissance.com

Tourin Palan Otel ****
Palandöken Kayak Merkezi
ERZURUM
Phone: 0(442) 317 07 02 - Fax: 0(442) 317 07 00
info@palanotel.com - www.palanotel.com

Hınısboğazı Mechanic Facilities

At the Palandöken-Hınısboğazı Ski Centre, there are one telecabin and seven chairlift facilities. Of these, the A, B and C lifts are 4CLD, while the other four have two seats, and all have been indicated on the map, with their characteristics being summarised below. [*]

Name of Facility	Length	Capacity
(TK) Telecabin	3237m.	1500 person per hour
(A) Lift	1456m.	2000 person per hour
(B) Lift	648m.	1800 person per hour
(C) Lift	1085m.	1800 person per hour
(E) Ejder Lift	1778m.	980 person per hour
(V) Valley Lift	1200m.	800 person per hour
(G) South Lift	1528m.	800 person per hour
(P) Polat Lift	1097m.	850 person per hour

Source: Turkish Ski Federation, 2011

(*) 4CLD : four-seat chairlift facility , 2CL : two-seat chairlift facility

KONAKLI SKI CENTRE

"Second Development Area"

The Konaklı Ski Areas are located to the south-west of the Erzurum city centre, within the administrative boundaries of the village of Konaklı. They are at a distance of 18 km. from the city centre, on the Çat Main Highway, within the 2250-3100 m. altitude belt. All of these slopes face the north, and while in normal winter conditions their lower parts receive 50-100 cm. of snow, their upper parts receive around 150 – 200 cm. of snow,

KONAKLI SKI CENTRE "Konaklı Village"

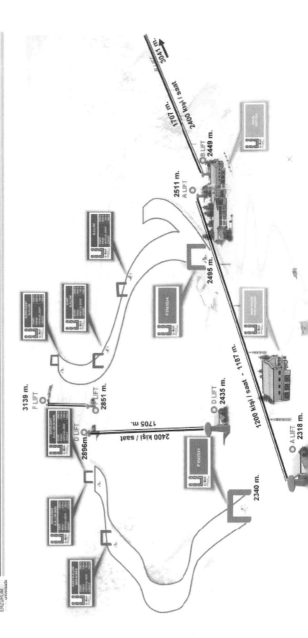

and they have a 150 day/year ski season. The most suitable time for skiing is the 10th December – 20th April period.

This area, which is suitable for Alpine skiing and tour skiing, is important for freestyle skiing and competitions as defined by F.I.S. standards.

The Alpine skiing competitions of the "Universiad – Erzurum 2011" winter games will be held in this area; with the nordic skiing and cross-country skiing and rifle shooting "Biathlon" being held at the Kandilli Area, and the ski jumping facilities and ice rink being set up in the Erzurum city centre.

As a first stage, the Slalom, Giant Slalom and Super Giant Slalom pistes and six four-seat chairlifts and also a "service building" for sportspersons and visitors were built at the Konaklı Ski Centre. "Artificial snow" facilities have been set up for all competition and freestyle skiing pistes.

The service building is sufficiently large and has the necessary characteristics, and has been planned so that cafe, cafeteria, ski sale and rental and ticket sale services can be provided in it. Five hotel investments for a total of 5,000 beds have been planned for the Konaklı Ski Centre.

The competition pistes at the Konaklı Ski Centre and the ski mechanic facilities have been indicated on the relevant map and detailed information about the mechanic facilities has been provided below.

Ski Mechanic Facilities

Name	Length	Carriage Capacity	Bevel
A Lift	1187m.	1200 person per hour	16%
B Lift	1707m.	2400 person per hour	25%
C Lift	1690m.	2400 person per hour	17%
D Lift	1705m.	2400 person per hour	27%
F Lift	708m.	1800 person per hour	41%
G Lift	1410m.	2400 person per hour	31%

Source: Turkish Ski Federation, 2011

Updated Information and Recommendations

The Palandöken "Hınısboğazı" Ski Centre is located to the south-east of the Erzurum city centre, on the northern slopes of Palandöken Mountain. The ski centre, which is situated within the 2200-3176 m. altitude belt, is at a distance of 5 km. from the city centre. The city of Erzurum is connected to Ankara and Istanbul by road, air and rail, and the ski centre is connected by highway to the city centre. As for the newly planned "Konaklı Ski Centre", it is on the "Çat road" at a distance of 18 km. from Erzurum.

In normal winter conditions, the ski season begins on 10th December and ends on 30th April, and as such it is "150/day/year". As for the northern slopes of the Büyükejder Hill, it offers the opportunity of skiing up to 15th - 20th June. In Palandöken, where the snow will in general have reached 150-200 cm. by March in the higher parts, the snow will be "powder snow" and sunny days will predominate as a result of the continental climate conditions.

At the Hınısboğazı Ski Centre there are in operation the four star, 630 bed "Dedeman Hotel", the 400-bed Palan Hotel and Polat Renaissance Hotel with around 1000 beds. In addition to these, there are another three hotels certified as touristic, in the city centre.

At the Palandöken Ski Centre there is a sufficient number of distinguished ski trainers. Beginners should take two hours of lessons for at least five days. The prices of individual or collective lessons change every year.

At the Palandöken "Hınısboğazı" Ski Centre there is one telecabin, five chairlifts, two teleski facilities, and an 80-room and 160-bed "Ski Training Centre," all of which are in continuous service.

There is the possibility of buying or renting all kinds of ski clothing and equipment both in the city centre and in the mountain hotels. Ski trainers should be consulted when buying or renting new equipment.

The hotels have doctors and health personnel. In case of accidents or injuries in the mountain, skip trainers provide first aid or transport on sledges. Skiers on Palandöken Mountain should not ski outside the compressed ski pistes, which are indicated by signs, and in particular should avoid deep snow bowls.

Teams wishing to do tour skiing should wait for clear and sunny weather and carry out such activities in the company of guides.

Detailed Information and Offices

Turkish Ski Federation
Türkocağı Cad. 29. Sk. No:4/9
Balgat - ANKARA
Phone: 0(312) 285 11 38 Fax: 0(312) 285 11 32
www. kayak.org.tr – info@kayak.org.tr

Culture and Tourism Directorate
Cemal Gürsel Cad. No:9, ERZURUM
Phone: 0(442) 235 09 25, Fax: 0(442) 233 07 71
iktm25@kultur.gov.tr

KARS - SARIKAMIŞ

Sarıkamış, which lies along the Erzurum-Kars railroad and highway, is at a distance of 60 km. from Kars, and of 150 km. from Erzurum. The Sarıkamış Cıbıltepe Ski Centre is one of Turkey's six main ski centres, set at an altitude of 2092–2634 m., surrounded by Scotch pine forests, and looks like a high and flat mountain, in comparison to its surroundings. While all the clearings in the forests in the near environs of Sarıkamış are particularly suitable for "ski runs" and "tour skiing" activities, Cıbıltepe (2634 m.) rising to the south of the Sarıkamış county seat, is suitable for Alpine skiing and freestyle skiing.

Sarıkamış and its surroundings consist of basaltic layers formed during the Tertiary Period as a result of "surface eruptions". This area, which was eroded and acquired a flat look under the influence of external forces, nowadays is a high plateau covered with "Scotch pine forests" and pastures. Sarıkamış and its surroundings, which are located within the scope of the Eastern Anatolian continental climate and which receive plenty of snow all through the winter, are an important area not just for winter sports and tourism, but also for their natural beauty.

Sarıkamış and its surroundings were first included within the scope of planning with the aim of evaluating their suitability for winter sports and tourism in 1976 and these studies were completed in 1979.

Snow Conditions and Ski Season

Sarıkamış and its surroundings located within the Eastern Anatolian continental climate belt, have temperate summers, and cold and snowy winters. According to long-term data from the Sarıkamış meteorology station, Sarıkamış and its surroundings are covered by snow for 142 days on average and the highest level of snow ever measured is 202 cm. In normal winter conditions, the lower parts of the "Cıbıltepe Ski Areas" receive 50-100 cm. of snow and its upper parts 100-150 cm.

The Sarıkamış Ski Centre has a "120 day/year" ski season. The ski areas around Sarıkamış, which in general are covered by "powder snow" all through winter, have conditions suitable for winter sports in the 10th December - 10th April period.

Name of Station: Sarıkamış
Altitude: 2092 m.

	I	II	III	IV	V	VI	VII	VIII	IX	X	XI	XII	Yıl
Average monthly temperature (C°)	-9	-9	4	2	8	12	15	15	10	4	0	-6	3
Sunny and partially sunny days/month	21	20	21	22	23	27	20	29	27	25	23	20	282
Average number of snow-covered days/month	31	28	28	14	-	-	-	-	-	1	9	27	142
Greatest thickness of snow-cover (cm.)	98	175	202	90	10	2	-	-	1	25	58	67	202
Average monthly relative humidity	80	78	79	77	74	70	68	66	66	73	78	80	74

Source: Bulletin of State Meteorology Affairs General Directorate.

CIBILTEPE SKI CENTRE

"First Development Area"

Cıbıltepe (2634 m.) rising to the south of the city at a distance of around 7 km. and covered with Scotch pine forests, has, thanks to its snowy slopes and ski pistes of various inclination and length, been opened for investments as the "First Development Area". Süphan Mountain (2909 m.), which from the point of view of its natural environment and ground is similar to Cıbıltepe and surroundings, has been declared to be the "Second Development Area", while the Hamamlı-Ağbaba Area has been declared "Third Development Area".

The "Cıbıltepe Ski Centre" set at the 2100-2600 m. altitude belt, is suitable not just for Alpine skiing and freestyle skiing but also tour skiing.

Since all the ski areas around Sarıkamış are set at altitudes higher than 2100 m., the centre approaches the height threshold for Nordic skiing male and female "ski run races" and "speed skating competitions".

Even though the ski areas in Sarıkamış and surroundings present some limitations in this respect, they also offer some advantages, especially as far as ability- and power-developing "performance" activities are concerned.

The old ski area at the Sarıkamış Ski Centre has been named the "Osman Yüce Ski Centre". As for the new ski centre, it has been developed on Cıbıltepe "Bayrak Tepe". In the old ski centre there is a 60-bed "Ski Training Centre" and a teleski facility.

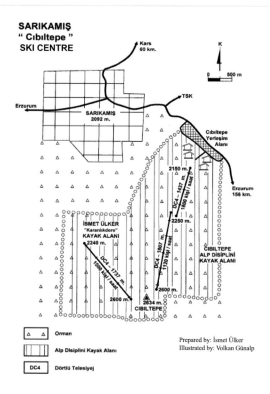

SARIKAMIŞ
" Cıbıltepe "
SKI CENTRE

△ △	Orman
(Alp Disiplini Kayak Alanı)	Alp Disiplini Kayak Alanı
DC4	Dörtlü Telesiyej

Prepared by: İsmet Ülker
Illustrated by: Volkan Günalp

On the Cıbıltepe Ski Centre, which was opened for new investments in 1992, there are three good quality hotels, a ski refuge, and three chairlifts.

The chairlift facilities serving the Cıbıltepe Ski Areas and their characteristics have been indicated on the map, and lodging facilities have been listed below. The four star, 285-bed Dedeman Hotel is under construction.

Lodging Establishments

Toprak Hotel *****
Cıbıltepe Mevkii Kayak Merkezi
Sarıkamış / Kars
Phone: 0(474) 413 41 11 - Fax: 0(474) 413 79 05
salessarikamishotel@toprak.com.tr
www.sarikamistoprakhotels.com

Çamkar Hotel ***
Cıbıltepe Mevkii Kayak Merkezi
Sarıkamış / Kars
Phone: 0(474) 413 65 65 – Fax: 0(474) 413 62 42
camkar@camkar.com – www.camkar.com

Kar Otel ***
Cıbıltepe Mevkii Kayak Merkezi
Sarıkamış / Kars
Phone: 0(474) 413 51 52 – Fax: 0(474) 413 50 51
www.sarikamis.com.tr

Osman Yüce Kayak Eğitim Merkezi
Gençlik ve Spor İl Müdürlüğü
Sarıkamış / Kars
Phone: 0(474) 413 81 43

Updated Information and Recommendations

The Sarıkamış Ski Centre is located on the Erzurum-Kars highway and railroad. It is at a distance of 60 km. from Kars, 150 km. from Erzurum and 50 km. from Kars airport. It is possible to reach the Sarıkamış Ski Centre on a daily basis from Istanbul or Ankara via the Erzurum or Kars airport.

The best skiing season for the Sarıkamış Ski Centre, which has a "120 day/year" season, and the ski pistes, which are in general covered with "powder snow", consists of the 20th December – 30th March period. At the Sarıkamış Ski Centre, which receives a lot of snow all through winter, the snow cover in general reaches 100-200 cm. Those wishing to do tour skiing in the surroundings of Sarıkamış should do so with a guide, and they should prefer clear and sunny days.

At the Cıbıltepe Ski Centre the three star Kar Hotel and Çamkar Hotel and the 330-bed, five star Toprak Hotel are in operation.

Distinguished ski trainers with certificates are active at the Cıbıltepe Ski Centre. There is the possibility of buying new ski clothing and equipment from the boutiques in both the Sarıkamış county centre and in the hotels. In addition to this, it is also possible to rent ski equipment under the supervision of a trainer.

Detailed Information and Offices

Turkish Ski Federation
Türkocağı Cad. 29. Sk. No:4/9, Balgat - ANKARA
Phone: 0(312) 285 11 38 - Fax: 0(312) 285 11 32
www. kayak.org.tr - info@kayak.org.tr

AREAS POTENTIALLY SUITABLE FOR WINTER SPORTS

Even though skiing is fast developing in Turkey, ski areas with conditions and locations suitable for winter sports have not yet been studied completely and sufficiently.

Antalya - Kızlarsivrisi, Bolkar Mountains - Aksaray - Hasan Mountain, Erzincan - Munzur Mountain, Iğdır - Korhan Plateau, Trabzon - Zigana Mountain and Uzungöl - Multat Plateau are the main of these potential ski areas.

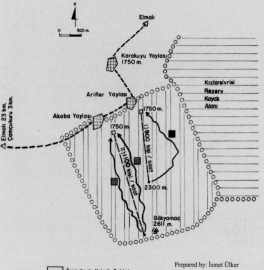

ANTALYA - BEYDAĞLARI
KIZLARSİVRİSİ SKI AREA

K

0   500 m.

Elmalı

Karakuyu Yaylası
1750 m.

Kızlarsivrisi
Rezerv
Kayak
Alanı

Arifler Yaylası

1750 m.

Akoba Yaylası

Elmalı 23 km.
Çamçukuru 3 km.

1750 m.

1) 900 kişi / saat

1) 1100 kişi / saat

2300 m.

Gökyamaç
2611 m.

Prepared by: İsmet Ülker

———— Öneri Kayak Mekanik Tesisleri

▨ Kayak Alanı

--- Stabilize Yol

ANTALYA – BEYDAĞLARI

Its ski areas are set on the highest and western part of the Beydağları, on the north-west and north-facing slopes of Kızlarsivrisi (3070 m.). These areas are covered with cedar and pine trees up to 1800 metres. Further up from this altitude is a topography with regular surfaces, covered with alpine meadows. These meadows on the 1800-2600 metre altitude belt have inclinations ranging between 30% and 75% and differences in height of up to 800 metres, with the result that their ski pistes for both Alpine skiing and freestyle skiing are up to olympic standards.

In normal winter conditions, this area will receive around 50-100 cm. of snow. Since the ski area is distant from the sea and subject to continental climate conditions, the snow will be of a sufficiently good quality. This area has a "120 day/year" ski season, which comprises the 20th December – 20th April period.

The ski area between the Akoba Plateau (1750 m.), the Arifler Plateau (1750 m.), the Gökyamaç Peak (2611 m.) and the Kızlarsivrisi (3070 m.) Peak, is at a distance of 140 km. from Antalya via Elmalı-Korkuteli, and of 120 km. from Kemer via Finike. Exiting the highway about 14 km. past Elmalı, you will reach the Çamçukuru Plateau after 10 km. and the Akoba Plateau after a further 2 km. The road is of compressed earth and fairly good.

It has been deemed necessary to give precedence and open up for investments the "2000 skier/day" capacity "Göktepe Ski Areas". The master plan proposals concerning the Kızlarsivrisi Ski Area have been indicated on the relevant map.

The proposed ski mechanic facilities indicated on the map and the ski pistes, will at first have a carrying capacity of around "2000 skiers/day", while the areas on the north of Kızlarsivrisi Mountain will have a potential usage of "3000 skiers/day".

The ski areas have olympic standard pistes for Alpine skiing and Nordic skiing and are suitable for activities like tour skiing etc.; and are also open for new investments.

BOLKAR MOUNTAINS

The Niğde-Bolkar Mountains Darboğaz-Meydan Ski Area is located approximately within the 2300-3300 m. altitude belt. This area is set to the south of the Darboğaz town in the county of Ulukışla in the province of Niğde, to the west of the Çiftehan Town-Maden Village, and on the northern slopes of the Bolkar

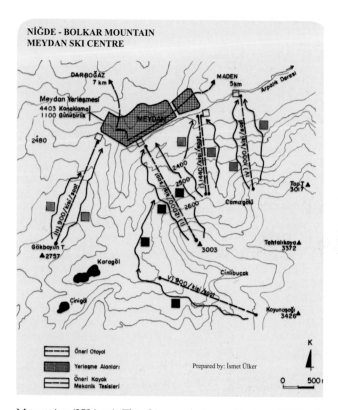

NİĞDE - BOLKAR MOUNTAIN
MEYDAN SKI CENTRE

Prepared by: İsmet Ülker

Mountains (3524 m.). The ski areas between Toptepe (3017 m.),
Tahtalıkaya (3372 m.) and Koyunaşağı Peak (3426 m.) to the East,
Eğerkaya (3347 m.), Erkaya (3308 m.) and Çinigöl to the south,
and Gökboyun (2750 m.) and Meydan Plateau (2300 m.) to the
west, cover an area of around 2000 hectares.

The Meydan Plateau, which is 16 km. from the Ankara-Adana
highway, 7 km. from Darboğaz and 5 km. from the village of
Çiftehan-Maden, is particularly suitable for Alpine skiing and
tour skiing. The ski pistes within the Bolkar Mountains, Meydan
Plateau Ski Areas have slopes of various different heights,
inclinations and lengths, and as such are up to international and
olympic standards.

These areas receive a lot of snow in winter, and in normal winter
conditions there will be 50-100 cm. of snow on the lower parts,
and 100-200cm. on the upper parts. The most suitable time for

skiing on the Meydan Plateau, which has a "150 day/year" ski season, is the 10th December – 20th April period. The lodging area and ski mechanic facilities planned for the Bolkar Mountains, "Meydan Plateau Ski Areas", have been indicated on the relevant map.

Five ski mechanic facilities have been planned for the Bolkar Mountains, Meydan Ski Areas. In relation to these facilities and using the SKCC formula, a capacity of "4403 skiers/day/ carrying" has been determined. Consequently, a 4,403-bed, 5,500-person ski centre expecting 1,100 daily visitors, has been proposed for the ski area.

Located 16 km. from the Adana-Ankara main highway and set on the northern slopes of the Bolkar Mountains, the ski area has competition and freestyle skiing pistes up to olympic standards. However, it must be developed in a planned way. This ski area is particularly important because it will attract people not only from Ankara and Çukurova, but also from the countries of the Middle East.

AKSARAY - HASAN MOUNTAIN

The ski areas on the northern and north-west slopes of Hasan Mountain (3268 m.) are within the boundaries of "Kargın Village". The "Hasan Mountain Ski Areas" are set at the 1800-2500 metre altitude belt, and their distance from Aksaray is 30 km.

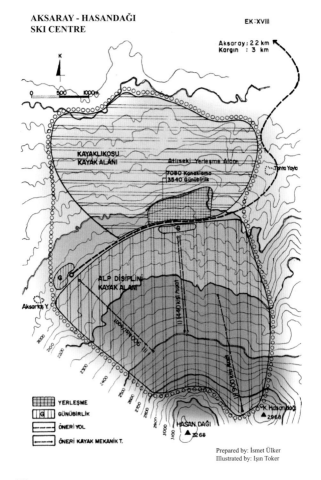

AKSARAY - HASANDAĞI SKI CENTRE

EK:XVIII

Aksaray : 22 km
Kargın : 3 km

KAYAKLIKOSU KAYAK ALANI

Atlıseki Yerleşme Alanı
7080 Konaklama
3540 Günübirlik

Tahta Yayla

ALP DİSİPLİNİ KAYAK ALANI

Aksaray Y.

HASAN DAĞI
▲ 3268

K. Hasandağı
▲ 2968

YERLEŞME
GÜNÜBİRLİK
ÖNERİ YOL.
ÖNERİ KAYAK MEKANİK T.

Prepared by: İsmet Ülker
Illustrated by: Işın Toker

These ski areas located to the south of the line joining Atlıseki in the east and Munamak Peak in the west and on the northern slopes of Hasan Mountain, are more suited for Alpine skiing, ski runs and tour skiing.

The 20th December-20th April period is best suited for skiing. Ski pistes have favourable conditions as far as length, height, inclination and the thickness of the snow cover are concerned. Average snow cover is 50-100 cm.

The ski mechanic facilities planned for the Aksaray-Hasan Mountain Ski Area have been indicated on the relevant map, and the "carrying/day/capacity" have been indicated below.

Planned teleski facility number I (double ascent)

$$\frac{1440 \times 500 \times 6}{4000} = 1080 \text{ skier / day}$$

Planned chairlift facility number II:

$$\frac{900 \times 650 \times 6}{4000} = 878 \text{ person / day}$$

Planned chairlift facility number III:

$$\frac{900 \times 350 \times 6}{4000} = 473 \text{ person / day}$$

According to the SKCC formula, the Hasan Mountain Ski Area has a total capacity of "2430/skier/day", and consequently a 2430-bed and 610-daily visitor capacity has been proposed.

Aksaray-Hasandağı should be considered in conjunction with the Ihlara Valley and the Cappadocia Area. This area offers "daily excursion" opportunities in the winter for all those lodging in the city of Aksaray and in its environs. On the Hasan Mountain there is a mountain and ski refuge with a capacity of around 60 beds. The importance of this establishment is that it offers lodgings for mountaineers and skiers.

ERZİNCAN-MUNZUR MOUNTAIN

In the province of Erzincan, apart from the "Sakaltutan Ski Centre", which is still used and which is of only local importance, the area suitable for winter sports at a national and international level is located on Munzur Mountains, Ergan Mountain (3258 m.) rising to the south of the Erzincan city centre.

The ski areas on the northern slopes (1800-2800 m.) of Ergan Mountain which is made up of limestone rocks, are suitable for Alpine skiing, while areas nearby are suitable for Nordic skiing and tour skiing.

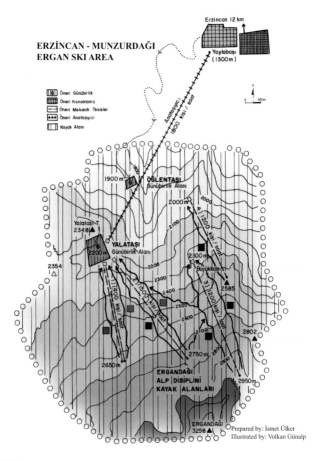

The north-facing parts of Ergan Mountain within the administrative boundaries of the village of Yaylabaşı, have a high potential value especially for Alpine skiing.

The "Yaylabaşı Village" at an altitude of around 1300 m. is connected to Erzincan over Çatalören by means of a tarmac road. The Çatalören-Erzincan distance is 8 km. while the Yaylabaşı Village is at a distance of 12 km. To the south of the ski areas there is the Kılıçkaya Stream and the Akbaba Peak (3462 m.), while to their north are the villages of Yaylabaşı and Türkmenoğlu.

The ski areas on the northern slopes of Ergandağı are devoid of forests and are covered with natural meadows.

The Ergan Mountain Ski Areas, which have natural ski pistes that are suitable for Alpine skiing up to olympic and international standards, have a ski season of around "150 day/year". According to local studies and research, in normal winter conditions the Ergan Mountain Ski Areas receive at least 50-100 cm. of snow. The best time for skiing is the 15th December -15th April period. A continental climate predominates in the area.

The map about the decisions and capacities concerning the Erzincan-Ergan Mountain ski areas have been indicated on the relevant map and have been explained below. The SKCC formula has been used for the determination of the "carrying/day/skier" capacity of the mechanic facilities and ski area.

ERGANDAĞI SKI AREA

Planned teleski facility number I (double ascent)

$$\frac{1440 \times 450 \times 6}{4000} = 972 \text{ skier / day}$$

Planned chairlift facility number II:

$$\frac{1550 \times 550 \times 6}{4000} = 1238 \text{ person / day}$$

Planned chairlift facility number III:

$$\frac{1200 \times 675 \times 6}{4000} = 1170 \text{ person / day}$$

Planned chairlift facility number IV:

$$\frac{1200 \times 580 \times 6}{4000} = 1044 \text{ person / day}$$

Four ski mechanic facilities and a total "4424 skier/day" carrying capacity have been proposed for the Erzincan, Munzur Mountain - Ergan Mountain Ski Area. In consideration of the assumption that there will be an intense usage of the Ergan Mountain Ski Area for daily excursions, a 1000-person daily usage capacity has been proposed. It is assumed that part of the hotels will be built in the Erzincan city centre and part in the village of Yaylabaşı.

IĞDIR KORHAN PLATEAU

The Korhan Plateau on the north-west slope of the Greater Ararat and to the north of the famous Küp Lake, at an altitude of 2000 m. has a topography that is suitable for both Alpine skiing and freestyle skiing, and also Nordic freestyle skiing.

The Korhan Plateau, which was used as a first campsite by A. Von Parrot, who was the first to climb the Greater Ararat in the summer, has not only Alpine ski pistes up to olympic standards, but also worldwide importance as a route for the ascent of the Greater Ararat.

The Korhan Plateau, which was first studied on-site on 15th September 2000, by a technical committee led by İsmet Ülker, is at a distance of 16 km. from the Iğdır-Doğubeyazıt main highway and 33 km. from Iğdır.

The ski areas on Korhan Plateau (2000-3000 m.) offer skiing at olympic standards from the point of view of the lengths, inclinations and heights of their pistes. Two chairlifts with a carrying capacity of "1200/person/hour" and a length of around 1750 m. and a mountain and winter sports centre with a "2500-3000 person/day" capacity has been planned for this area.

The investments planned for the "Korhan Plateau", which is of both national and international importance, for both mountaineering, and winter sports, have not yet been carried out. Of the planned facilities, only a "mountain and ski refuge" have been completed.

TRABZON – ZİGANA MOUNTAIN

The Zigana Mountain Ski Areas are located within the province of Gümüşhane, on the north slopes of Zigana Mountain; to the east of the Old Zigana Pass, and within the 1900-2500 m. altitude belt. The ski areas are at a distance of 40 km. from Gümüşhane, of 60 km. from Trabzon and of 30 km. from Maçka; and are close enough to Trabzon for people from this city to come for daily excursions.

The Zigana Mountain Ski Area has no infrastructure problem concerning matters like transport or electricity and its "Yurt Plateau" where the ski pistes are located, has been included within the scope of planning. There is no danger of avalanches or land slides in the ski area. The ski area is covered with pastures with regular surfaces.

The Zigana Mountain Ski Areas is up to olympic standards as far as Slalom, Giant Slalom and Super Giant Slalom competitions are concerned, from the point of view of the lengths, inclinations and height differences of the pistes. Zigana Mountain in general receives around 100-200 cm. of snow and as such it is suitable also for winter tourism and freestyle skiing and is particularly important for Trabzon. In normal winter conditions,

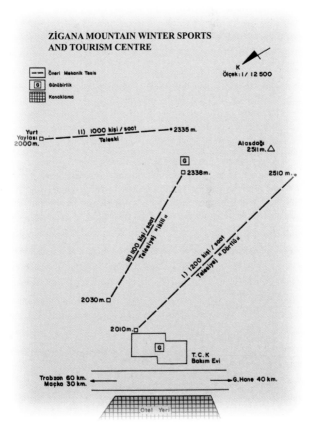

the Zigana Mountain Ski Areas have a "100-120/day/year" ski season, and the best time for skiing is the 20th December – 30th March period: Usage proposals (determined according to the SKCC formula) for the Zigana Mountain winter sports centre, which has ski pistes suitable for both freestyle skiing and competitive skiing, have been indicated below and on the map.

Planned chairlift facility number I:

$$\frac{1200 \times 500 \times 6}{4000} = 900 \text{ person / day}$$

Planned teleski or chairlift facility number II:

$$\frac{1000 \times 335 \times 6}{4000} = 502 \text{ person / day}$$

Planned chairlift facility number III:

$$\frac{1100 \times 308 \times 6}{4000} = 508 \text{ person / day}$$

The Mountain Ski Centre is within the scope of daily excursions from both Trabzon and Gümüşhane. It is for this reason that it has been assumed that half of the total expected "skier/day" usage capacity will be used by people on daily excursions and the other half by people staying the night. There is also the possibility of staying in good quality lodging establishments in Trabzon or Maçka.

The Eastern Black Sea Area is becoming more important for tourism and mountain and winter tourism activities are acquiring precedence. This centre, which has olympic level ski pistes, is important from the point of view of "year round tourism" and of the "differentiation of tourism" in the Eastern Black Sea Area, and in particular in the Trabzon and Maçka areas.

UZUNGÖL – MULTAT PLATEAU

Trabzon-Uzungöl and its environs is both a tourism centre, and an area with a high potential for winter sports and tourism.

Uzungöl in the Trabzon-Çaykara county is at an altitude of 1150m. while the mountains surrounding it have altitudes ranging between 1900 and 3195 m. A new highway has been built connecting Uzungöl, which is at a distance of 40 km. from the Trabzon-Rize coastal road, of 65 km. from Rize and of 80 km. from Trabzon.

In recent years Uzungöl has become famous as an "Eco tourism" centre. There is the possibility of turning Uzungöl into both a "tourism centre" and a nationally important "winter sports centre".

In a way, the Kaçkar Mountains, which occupy a great part of the Eastern Black Sea Area, begin from the south of Uzungöl. The highest part of this area is Karakaya (3193 m.). This area, which contains high altitude glacier lakes "cirques", is very attractive from the points of view of mountaineering, high altitude mountain treks and tour skiing. In this area, which in a way is a "mountain and nature park", there are high altitude glacier lakes like Karagöl (2750 m.), Balık Lake (2600 m.) and Aygır Lake (2700 m.).

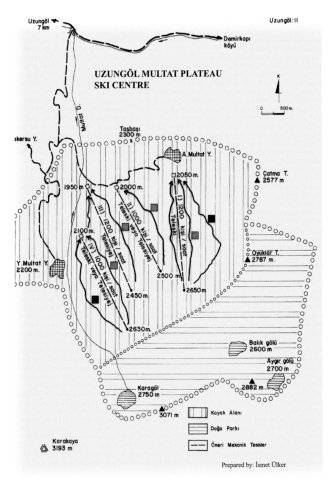

Prepared by: İsmet Ülker

Areas suitable for winter sports and tourism, are concentrated in three parts. "Multat Plateau" rising to the south of Uzungöl is the most important ski centre. Multat Plateau is located to the south of Uzungöl, and to the north and north-east of Karagöl Mountain (3195 m.). The ski areas to the south of Lower Multat Plateau are at a distance of 10 km. from Uzungöl. The "Multat Plateau Ski Areas", the road to which is open only in summer, are located within the 1900-2800 m. altitude belt.

The ski areas, which begin from the upper limit of forests on the Lower Multat Plateau, have inclinations ranging between 30 % and 60 %, differences of height of more than 800 metres and lengths of more than 3-4 km. and as such are up to olympic ski piste standards. In the ski areas there is no risk of avalanches of land slides, which are typical of the area.

According to on site studies and observations, in normal winter conditions Multat Plateau and the surrounding areas receive 100-200 cm. of snow. Multat Plateau has a ski season of around "150/day/year". The 10th December – 10th April period is the best time for "winter sports".

Multat Plateau is a candidate to become an important winter sports and tourism centre of the near future. Evaluations about this area have been indicated on the relevant map and below.

Planned teleski facility number I (double ascent)

$$\frac{1200 \times 600 \times 6}{4000} = 1080 \text{ skier / day}$$

Planned chairlift facility number II:

$$\frac{1000 \times 500 \times 6}{4000} = 750 \text{ person / day}$$

Planned chairlift facility number III:

$$\frac{1200 \times 500 \times 6}{4000} = 900 \text{ person / day}$$

Planned chairlift facility number IV:

$$\frac{1000 \times 550 \times 6}{4000} = 825 \text{ person / day}$$

The "Uzungöl-Multat Plateau winter sports and tourism centre" has according to the SKCC calculation, a usage capacity of around "3500 skier/day". All of the necessary lodging establishments could be built at Uzungöl, while the facilities serving the needs of daily excursions could be set up on Multat Plateau. In this way, the lodging establishments in Uzungöl, which are used intensively in the summer, could be used year round. However, for this to be possible, a road should be built connecting Uzungöl and Multat Plateau (10 km.), and this road should be included in the "snow clearing and winter maintenance" programme.

In addition to these general principles, it is also possible to build a couple of mountain lodges on the Lower Multat Plateau and to have these hotels used for both winter and summer tourism.

WINTER SPORTS INSTITUTIONS IN TURKEY

Turkish Ski Federation
Türkocağı Cad. 29. Sk. No: 4/9
Balgat - ANKARA
Phone: 0(312) 285 11 31 - Fax: 0(312) 285 11 32

Ministry of Culture and Tourism
Tanıtma Genel Müdürlüğü İnönü Bulvarı No:5
Bahçelievler - ANKARA
Phone: 0(312) 213 17 85 - Fax: 0(312) 213 68 97
info@kultur.gov.tr

Travel Agencies Organising Winter Sports Tours

TEMPO TURİZM
Tunalıhilmi Caddesi, Binnaz Sok. 1/4
Kavaklıdere - ANKARA
Phone: 0(312) 428 20 96, Fax: 0(312) 426 16 70
www.tempotour.com.tr,
e-mail: tempo@tempotur.com.tr

MNG TURİZM Cumhuriyet Caddesi No:145
Harbiye - İSTANBUL
Phone: 444 20 00
www.mngturizm.com

DETUR Abdiipekçi Caddesi No:77/2
Maçka - İSTANBUL
Phone: 0(212) 343 88 77
e-mail: detur@detur.com.tr

ETSTUR Bağdat Caddesi No:69/13
Kızıltoprak - İSTANBUL
Phone: 0(216) 542 99 99
www.etstour.com

SETUR Cumhuriyet Caddesi No:69
Harbiye - İSTANBUL
Phone: 0(212) 230 03 36 – 0(212) 444 07 38

Mountaineering and Ski Equipment Sales Points

Alpinist – Doğa Sporları
Dikmen Caddesi No: 508/A Dikmen ANKARA
Phone: 0(312) 475 13 90
www.alpinist.com.tr

Toros - Kamp Ceyhun
Atıf Kansu Caddesi 43. Sk.No: 2/C
Balgat - ANKARA
Phone: 0(312) 284 60 10
www.toroskamp.com

Sport - Art
Arjantin Caddesi No:6/1
Kavaklıdere - ANKARA
Phone: 0(312) 427 61 92
e-posta: sportart@superonline.com

Karspor
Turan Güneş Bulvarı No:47/E
Çankaya - ANKARA
Phone: 0(312) 438 81 01
www.karspor.com

Adrenalin
Büyük Beşiktaş Çarşısı No:19
Beşiktaş - İSTANBUL
Phone: 0(212) 260 60 02
e-mail: adrenalin@com.tr

Slalom - Sport
Bağdat Caddesi No:368/10
Şaşkınbakkal - İSTANBUL
Phone: 0(216) 368 77 28
www.slalomsport.com

Arlbergsport
Sivas Caddesi, Birkan Sokak No: 17/ B, KAYSERİ
Phone: 0(352) 222 47 16
e-mail: arlbergsport@hotmail.com

Karspor
Cumhuriyet Caddesi No:16
ERZURUM
Phone: 0(442) 235 66 65
www.karspor.com

Ski Clubs

Bursa Ski Club
Haşim İşcan Cad. No:10
Osmangazi - BURSA
Phone: 0(224) 224 05 01
e-mail: ilmo@ilmo.com.tr

Hacılar Mountaineering and Winter Sports Club
Belediye Çarşısı No:9
Hacılar - KAYSERİ
Phone: 0(352) 442 24 46, Fax: 0(352) 442 35 76
www.hadak.org, hadak@hadak.org.

Sarıkamış Ski and Sports Club
Belediye İşhanı Kat:3
Sarıkamış - KARS
Phone: 0(474) 413 67 03

Erzurum Ski Club
Palandöken Kayak Tesisleri, ERZURUM
Phone: 0(442) 234 73 25, Gsm: 0(532) 334 65 60
info@erzurumkayakkulubu.com

Doğu Anadolu
Akay Mountaineering and Winter Sports Club
İsmet İnönü Caddesi No:49, ERZURUM
Phone: 0(442) 233 25 89
info@akaydagcilik.com

GLOSSARY

This section contains definitions of geological terms as well as information concerning proper names. The proper names include those of the first geologists to conduct studies in our high mountainous regions; the first mountain climbers to ascend our highest peaks during summer and winter; athletes who have contributed to the sport of Turkish mountain climbing, and provincial governors and other local administrators.

Atatepe: The highest peak of Greater Mount Ararat (5,137 m.), glacier-covered, located in the middle of the SE-NW summit line. Named after Mustafa Kemal ATATÜRK, it is the highest point of the Anatolian Peninsula.

Akıntepe: A summit located on the Niğde, Toros-Aladağları (3610 m.). It is named after Rasim Akın, a headmaster of Ankara-Çankaya Primary School who was an active mountaineer between the years 1940 and 1960, and who contributed to the promotion of Turkish Mountaineering.

Albayrak Glacier: A mountain glacier located on the northern slope of the Greater Ararat Mountain; it hangs down towards the Cenennemdere Valley. It is named after physical geographer Gülay Albayrak, who was part of the Elazığ climbing team, led by İsmet Ülker on 17th August 1973, which was the first to make the ascent to the top of the Greater Ararat (after Yıldız Değirmencioğlu on the same day).

Aloktepe: A summit (3474 m.) located on the Hakkari Sat Mountains, named after mountaineer and mountain photographer Ersin Alok.

Akınalan: The name of the station area at the Palandöken Mountains-Hınısboğazı Ski Centre. A settlement area named after Arif Akın, former director of Erzurum Province Youth and Sports, who served Turkish athletics and especially the Turkish Skiing for 35 years.

Atalay Glacier: A mountain glacier embedded on the southwestern slope of the Greater Ararat. It is named after Retired Colonel Şahap Atalay, who contributed to the international fame of Mount Ararat and served as a guide to the Frenchman F. Navara and American researcher J. Libby on their quest to find Noah's Ark on the Greater Ararat.

Ayder Plateau: A famous plateau and thermal spring centre of the Eastern Black Sea Region located at the entrance point to the Kaçkar Mountains (1250 m.) within the borders of the Çamlıhemşin county of Rize Province.

Mount Barut: A subsidiary volcanic mountain (2509 m.) rising on the northeastern slope of Mount Erciyes. Known locally as 'Lifos', it is named after the teacher Muharrem Barut, which made many ascents and led numerous convoys up Mount Erciyes between 1940 and 1960, and who also wrote poems and books about Mount Erciyes.

Bobek Summit: A peak (3980 m.) rising on the Hakkari-Cilo mountains. It is named after Dr. Hans Bobek, a geographer from Berlin University who conducted the first scientific studies of the Cilo-Sat mountains in 1937 and introduced this mountainous area to Europe.

Bozkurt Glacier: Mountain glacier embedded on the western slope of the Greater Ararat. Named after Dr. Bozkurt Ergör, a pioneer of mountaineering as a sport in Turkey in accordance with modern techniques who performed the first 'winter ascent' up Mount Ararat on 21st February 1970, and who was a founding member of the Turkish Mountaineering Federation and served as president of the federation for two terms.

Cehennemdere: An approximately 2000 metre-deep landslide valley located on the northern slope of the Greater Ararat. A 'nuclues glacier' measuring 5 km. in length is located on the floor of the valley.

Çakmak Summit: A summit (4767 m.) rising in the northwestern part of the Greater Ararat, on the peak line. It is named after Marshall Fevzi Çakmak, a commander during the War of Independence and comrade in arms of Mustafa Kemal Atatürk and İsmet İnönü.

Çeki Glacier: A mountain glacier embedded on the southwestern slope of the Greater Ararat. It is named after the famous composer Gültekin Çeki, who served as president of the Turkish Mountaineering and Winter Sports Federation for a period of 17 years, and who was part of the team that successfully ascended the Greater Ararat in 1954.

Erinç Summit: The second highest peak (4116 m.) on the Hakkari-Cilo Mountains. It is named after the famous scientist and geographer Prof. Dr. Sırrı Erinç, who conducted physical geographical studies on the Cilo Mountains in 1948 and contributed to the promotion of this mountainous region. (The same peak is known to western researchers as 'Suppadurek'.)

Erinç Glacier: A mountain glacier measuring approximately 4 km. in length, embedded on the northern slopes of Erinç Summit.

Gez Glacier: A mountain glacier located on the eastern slope of the Greater Ararat. Named after mountain guide and mountaineering trainer Muzaffer Erol Gez, who was a founding member of the Turkish Mountaineering Federation and the first to make the ascent to the peaks of the Greater Ararat from the eastern direction.

Heveg: A mountain village and pasture settlement located in the district of Yusufeli in Artvin Province, Heveg is the best location from which to approach and enter the Kaçkar Mountains from the south. The village is known today as 'Yaylalar'.

İnönü Summit: A summit (5122 m.) rising on the eastern part of the Greater Ararat, on the mountain's peak line. It is named after İsmet İnönü, second president of the Turkish Republic, commander during the War of Independence, and comrade in arms of Mustafa Kemal Atatürk

İzbırak Glacier: The largest mountain glacier in Turkey, located on the northeastern slope of Uludoruk 'Reşko' Summit (4136 m.) in the Hakkari-Cilo Mountains. Named after the famous geographer and scientist Prof. Dr. Reşat İzbırak, who conducted the first physical geographical studies of the Cilo Mountains in 1944 and, after studying the glacier in question on-site, published the first book about this mountainous region.

Karaduman: Name of the settlement located at the Hınısboğazı Skiing Centre on Mount Palandöken. Named after former governor of Erzurum, MP from Trabzon and Speaker of the Turkish Parliament, Necmettin Karaduman.

Karst Morphology: A geological term used to describe areas in flat or mountainous regions in which formations such as karrens, sinkholes, dolines, caves, etc. made of soluble limestone rock are found.

Karnıyarık Volcano: An auxiliary volcano and crater with a protruding chimney, its mouth still open in the southern section, located at a height of approximately 2500 m. on the southeastern slope of the Greater Ararat.

Karnıyarık Glacier: A mountain glacier consisting of two parts and extending from the peak of the Mount Ararat towards the auxiliary volcano of the same name.

Keten Summit: The new name of the Lesser Mount Erciyes (3703 m.). Named after geologist Prof. İhsan Keten, member of the Turkish Scientific Council, in his memory. Formerly known as 'Safrakaya'.

Kurt Mountain: A peak (3752 m.) rising in the western part of the Cilo Mountains, which European mountaineers refer to as 'Kisara'. Named after Asım Kurt, an athlete who was the head of the Turkish team that conducted the first climb and research on the Cilo Mountains in 1944, and who also acted as President of the Turkish Mountaineering and Winter Sports Federation in 1944-1966.

Küllahçı: A peak (3396 m.) that rises to the east of Bay Lake, on the Hakkari-Sat Mountains. named after photographic artist Necmettin Küllahçı, who traveled the Cilo-Sat Mountains and contributed to the promotion of the region.

Moraine: An accumulation of boulders and other rough stones, generally in the form of covers or levees, which are usually seen at the edges of glaciers and form in those areas where glaciers have melted.

Mount Yücedağ: Name of the skiing centre located in the northwestern part of the centre of the county of Sarkamış. Named after National Skier Osman Yüce, who originates from Sarıkamış and was part of the Turkish National Skiing Team from 1950 until 1964.

Omurtak Glacier: A mountain glacier located on the northwestern slopes of the Greater Ararat. Named after Salih Omurtak, a commander who served in the War of Independence and who served in the region.

Öğütçen: A summit (3311 m.) that rises on the south of Gevaruk Plateau in the Hakkari-Sat Mountains. Named after Hüseyin Öğütçen, former Governor of Hakkari and İzmir.

Özgüdek Summit: A summit (3620 m.) which rises to the north of Mount Cebel, in the Niğde-Taurus Aladağları Mountains. Named after former governor of Niğde and mountain-lover Ünal Özgüdek.

Özdirek Summit: A summit which rises to the southwest of Serpil Village, on the Hakkari-Cilo Mountains, and which Western mountaineers like to refer to as 'Belkıs'. Named Özdirek in memory of Muzaffer Özdemir, who, together with Kemal Çapa, was the first to make a winter ascent to the Reşko peak (4136 m.), on 5th March 1982.

Öz Summit: A summit (3675 m.) on the Hakkari-Sat Mountains. Named after mountain guide and mountaineering trainer Metin Öz, who conducted the first climb up the summit Çatalkaya, the highest peak of the Sat Mountains.

Parrot Glacier: A mountain glacier located on the northwestern slopes of the Greater Ararat. Named after German scientist A. von Parrot, who was the first to climb the Greater Ararat in 1829.

Perikartını: Lava flow and basalt rubble bed located on the northern slopes of Mount Erciyes. Such rock and rubble-covered areas are known locally as 'kartın'.

Şirin Lake: A glacial lake located on the northern slope of the Kızılkaya Peak (3725 m.) of the Niğde-Taurus Aladağları Mountains. A mountain and glacial lake the identification of which was first identified by İsmet Ülker (1964) and which bears the name of his daughter Şirin Ülker.

Sönmez Summit: Mountain peak (3860 m.) rising amongst the Rize-Kaçkar Mountains. Named after mountain guide and mountaineering trainer Sönmez Targan, who performed the first ascent to Kavron Peak (3932 m.) on 9th January 1974 and also served as the leader of the Turkish Mountaineering Group.

Türkünal Summit: Summit (3540 m.) which rises to the South of Mount Kurt, amongst the Hakkari-Cilo Mountains. Named after geologist Dr. Süleyman Türjünal, who conducted the first geological studies on the Cilo and Sat Mountains on behalf of MTA.

Ülkeroğlu Glacier: Mountain and valley glacier embedded on the southern slopes of the Greater Ararat. Named after İsmet Ülker, who was the first person to conduct studies on the volcanism and glacier morphology on the Greater Mount Ararat; who climbed the Greater Ararat five times for the purposes of mountaineering and conducting research; a founding member and president of the Turkish Mountaineering Federation (1966); head of the nation skiing team that made the first ascent up the Greater Ararat; and former president of the Skiing Federation (1972-76).

Yalçınlar Summit: Summit (3791 m.) of the Kaçkar-Kavrun Mountains. Named after Prof. Dr. İsmail Yalçınlar, who conducted physical geographical studies on the southern part of the Kaçkar Mountains which lie in the province of Artvin and who has published articles on the topic. Formerly known as 'Kardovit' (3791 m.).

Yıldız Glacier: Mountain glacier hanging on the northern side of the Greater Ararat, from the summit area down towards Cehennemdere Valley. Named after Yıldız Değirmencioğlu, who was the first to climb the Greater Ararat, on 17th August

1973 (before Gülay Albayrak on the same date), as part of the Manisa Mountaineering Team, under the leadership of Ertuğrul Dayıoğlu.

REFERENCES

AMELUNG, W., Prof. Dr. Medizinische Klimatologie, Dreikronnen Druck u. Verlag, Effern Bei Köln: 1976.

AYDINGÜN, H., Aladağlar, Redhouse Yayınevi, 1987.

BLUMENTHAL, M., Ağrı Volkanı ve Sedimanter Çevresinin Dağları' in İstanbul Üniversitesi Fen Fakültesi Mecmuası, Seri B, 1959.

ERGÖR, B., DAĞCILIK Anılar - Belgeler, Hasat Yayınları, 2001.

ERİNÇ, S., Dr., Kaçkar Dağı Grubunda Diluvial ve Bugünkü Glusyasyon in İstanbul Üniversitesi Fen Fakültesi Mecmuası, Seri B, 1949.

ERİNÇ, S., Dr., Doğu Anadolu Coğrafyası. İstanbul Üniversitesi Edebiyat Fakültesi Coğrafya Enstitüsü No: 15, 1953.

FINDIK, T., Kaçkar Dağları, Homer Kitabevi, Istanbul: 2001.

FINDIK, T., Tanrıların Tahtına Yolculuk, Everest Tırmanışının Hikayesi, Meteksan Sistem Yayınları, Istanbul: 2002.

GÜNER, Y., ŞAROĞLU, F., Doğu Anadolu'da Kuvaterner Volkanizması ve Jeotermal Enerji Açısından Önemi, Türkiye 7. Petrol Kongresi, TMMOB, Ankara: 1987.

TÜZEL, Ö., ALADAĞLAR, Trans. Tunç Fındık, Homer

T.M.M.O.B. Jeoloji Mühendisleri Odası Yayını, Istanbul: 1980.

İZBIRAK, R., Dr., Cilo Dağı ve Hakkari İle Van Gölü Çevresinde Coğrafya Araştırmaları, Anıl Matbaası, Istanbul: 1951.

MAHRUKİ, N., Everest'te İlk Türk, Yapı Kredi Yayınları, first edition, Istanbul: 1995.

ONUR, A., Dr., Türkiye'de Kar Yağışları, Ankara Üniversitesi, D.T.C.F. Fiziki Coğrafya Kürsüsü, Ankara: 1964.

SOMUNCU, M., Erciyes Dağının Jeolojisi ve Jeomorfolojisi, D.T.C.F. Fiziki Coğrafya ve Jeoloji Kürsüsü Ana Bilim Dalı, M.A. thesis, Ankara: 1984.

TEKELİ, O., AKSAY A., ÜRGÜN B., Türkiye Jeoloji Haritası 1/100.000 Kozan Paftası, M.T.A. Yayını, 1967.

TÜRKÜNAL, S., Dr., Doğu ve Güneydoğu Anadolu'nun Jeolojisi. T.M.M.O.B. Jeoloji Mühendisleri Odası Yayını-8, 1980.

TÜRKÜNAL, S., Dr., Türkiye'nin Sı· ·dağları ve Dağları. Kitabevi, Istanbul: 2001.

ÜLKER, İ., Cilo Dağlarında Glasyal Morfoloji, Ankara Üniversitesi D.T.C.F. Coğrafya ve Jeoloji Kürsüsü, Thesis, Ankara: 1963.

ÜLKER, İ., Büyük Ağrı Dağında Volkanik Şekiller, Ankara Üni. D.T.C.F. Fiziki Coğrafya ve Jeoloji Kürsüsü, B.A. Thesis, Ankara: 1964.

ÜLKER, İ., GÜRMAN S., MADANOĞLU, R., GÜNGÖR, E., Erzurum-PALANDÖKEN ve Kars-SARIKAMIŞ Kayak Merkezleri 1/25.000 Ölçekli Nazım İmar Planları Raporu, Turizm ve Tanıtma Bakanlığı, Ankara: 1979.

ÜLKER, İ., Turizm Sektöründe Doğal Kaynaklardan Yararlanma, 2. Türkiye İktisat Kongresi, Turizm Bakanlığı, Bakanlık Bildirisi, İzmir: 1981.

ÜLKER, İ., S., ÖRÜKLÜ, Ö., ORÇUN, S.,ÖZTÜRKCAN, N., Kayseri-Erciyes Dağı, Bolu-Köroğlu Dağı 1/25.000 Ölçekli Nazım İmar Planı Raporları, Turizm ve Tanıtma Bakanlığı, Ankara: 1981.

ÜLKER, İ., Türkiye'de Dağ Turizmi ve Kış Sporları, Turizm Bankası, Teksir Yayın, 1983: Ankara.

ÜLKER, İ., Dağlarda Kırk Yıl, BRC Matbaası, Ankara: 2002.

ÜLKER, İ., Dağlarımız, Publication of the Republic of Turkey Ministry of Culture and Tourism, Grafiker Matbaası, Ankara: 2007.